NIV개정

약속의 성경

영어 요절 따라쓰기

이　　름 : ______________________

시작한 날 : ______________________

끝마친 날 : ______________________

너희가 성경에서 영생을 얻는 줄 생각하고
성경을 연구하거니와
이 성경이 곧 내게 대하여 증언하는 것이니라

요한복음 5장 39절

약속의 성경 영어 요절 따라쓰기 소개

성경은 하나님의 약속으로 가득합니다. 약속의 성경 영어 요절 따라쓰기는 우리 자녀들이 예수님을 믿는 믿음 안에서 천국에 대한 확실한 소망을 가지고 살아가기를 바라는 마음으로 만든 책입니다. 이 책은 창세기부터 요한계시록까지의 말씀 중에서 핵심적인 내용들을 간추렸습니다. 또한 그 말씀이 의미하는 바를 정확하게 전달하기 위하여 한 절 한 절 이어 여러 구절로 구성했습니다. 약속의 성경 영어 요절 따라쓰기를 쓰면서 하나님의 약속들을 마음판에 새기며 세상에서 성령의 능력으로 빛과 소금이 되기를 원합니다.

약속의 성경 영어 요절 따라쓰기 특징

1. 영어 성경이 없어도 영어 성경을 읽고 쓰는 것이 즐겁습니다.
2. 영어 성경을 쓰면서 성경의 맥락이 쉽게 이해되어 성경 암송이 쉽습니다.
3. 영어 성경을 쓰면서 하나님의 약속들을 생각하며, 기대하게 됩니다.
4. 영어 성경을 쓰면서 하나님의 깊은 사랑을 깨닫게 됩니다.
5. 영어 성경을 쓰면서 약속에 신실하신 하나님을 발견하게 됩니다.
6. 영어 성경을 쓰면서 하나님의 자녀로 천국에 대한 확실한 소망을 갖게 됩니다.
7. 영어 성경을 쓰면서 좋은 글씨체를 갖게 됩니다.
8. 각 페이지마다 숙어와 예문, 각 주제의 단어 뜻풀이를 통해 영어 해석에 도움이 됩니다.
9. 부록에 수록된 원어민 발음과 한국어 성경(개역개정)을 통해 영어성경이 쉽게 읽어집니다.

말씀을 따라쓰기 전에 알아 두세요.

1. 말씀을 쓰기 전 성령님의 도움으로 영어 성경을 깨닫게 해 달라고 기도해 보세요.
2. 쓰면서 큰 소리로 따라 읽으세요. 암송의 효과를 얻을 수 있어요.
3. 모르는 단어는 함께 수록되어 있는 뜻을 찾아보세요.
   영어 성경을 쉽게 이해하게 해 줄 거예요.
4. 쓴 만큼의 날짜를 꼭 적어 보세요.
   얼마나 규칙적으로 영어 성경쓰기를 했는지 알 수 있습니다.
5. 영어 성경을 쓰고 난 후 부모님이나 선생님께 보여드려 검사를 받으세요.
   부모님과 선생님은 어린이에게 하고 싶은 말이나 축복의 문구를 써 주시면 큰 힘이 됩니다.

contents

contents

contents

년 월 일

The righteous will live by faith.

Romans 1 : 16~17 16 For I am not
ashamed of the gospel, because it is the
power of God that brings salvation to
everyone who believes: first to the Jew,
then to the Gentile. 17 For in the gospel
the righteousness of God is revealed—a
righteousness that is by faith from first
to last, just as it is written: "The right-
eous will live by faith."

Mark 9 : 23~24 23 " 'If you can'?" said
Jesus. "Everything is possible for one
who believes." 24 Immediately the boy's
father exclaimed, "I do believe; help me

be ashamed of 부끄러워하다
I am ashamed of my ignorance. 나는 내 무지가 부끄럽다.

overcome my unbelief!"

Mark 16 : 17~20

17 And these signs
will accompany those who believe: In
my name they will drive out demons;
they will speak in new tongues; 18 they
will pick up snakes with their hands; and
when they drink deadly poison, it will
not hurt them at all; they will place their
hands on sick people, and they will get
well." 19 After the Lord Jesus had spoken
to them, he was taken up into heaven and
he sat at the right hand of God. 20 Then the
disciples went out and preached every-
where, and the Lord worked with them
and confirmed his word by the signs
that accompanied it.

not (do) at all 일절 …하지 않다
This picture is not at all like. 이 사진은 조금도 닮지 않았다.

년 월 일

John 1 : 12~13

12 Yet to all who did
receive him, to those who believed in
his name, he gave the right to become
children of God— 13 children born not
of natural descent, nor of human deci-
sion or a husband's will, but born of
God.

John 3 : 16

16 For God so loved
the world that he gave his one and only
Son, that whoever believes in him shall
not perish but have eternal life.

John 12 : 44~50

44 Then Jesus cried
out, "Whoever believes in me does not
believe in me only, but in the one who
sent me. 45 The one who looks at me is
seeing the one who sent me. 46 I have

believe in …을 믿다
I just don't believe in false hope. 나는 헛된 희망은 믿지 않아요.

년 월 일

come into the world as a light, so that
no one who believes in me should stay
in darkness.
47 "If anyone hears my words
but does not keep them, I do not judge
that person. For I did not come to judge
the world, but to save the world.
48 There
is a judge for the one who rejects me
and does not accept my words; the very
words I have spoken will condemn
them at the last day.
49 For I did not
speak on my own, but the Father who
sent me commanded me to say all that
I have spoken.
50 I know that his com-
mand leads to eternal life. So whatever
I say is just what the Father has told me
to say."

lead to …로 이어지다
Too much drink can lead to a host of ills. 과음은 여러 가지 질병을 유발할 수 있다.

년 월 일

John 17 : 3~5 3 Now this is eter-
nal life: that they know you, the only
true God, and Jesus Christ, whom you
have sent. 4 I have brought you glory on
earth by finishing the work you gave me
to do. 5 And now, Father, glorify me in
your presence with the glory I had with
you before the world began.

John 20 : 27~29 27 Then he said to
Thomas, "Put your finger here; see my
hands. Reach out your hand and put it
into my side. Stop doubting and be-
lieve." 28 Thomas said to him, "My Lord
and my God!" 29 Then Jesus told him,
"Because you have seen me, you have
believed; blessed are those who have

put it into …에 넣다
You can put it into your pocket. 여러분은 그것을 주머니에 넣을 수 있다.

not seen and yet have believed."

Romans 3 : 29~31

29 Or is God the God
of Jews only? Is he not the God of Gen-
tiles too? Yes, of Gentiles too, 30 since
there is only one God, who will justify
the circumcised by faith and the uncir-
cumcised through that same faith. 31 Do
we, then, nullify the law by this faith? Not
at all! Rather, we uphold the law.

Romans 10 : 9~10

9 If you declare with
your mouth, "Jesus is Lord," and believe
in your heart that God raised him from
the dead, you will be saved. 10 For it is
with your heart that you believe and are
justified, and it is with your mouth that
you profess your faith and are saved.

raise from …에서 올리다
Slowly raise the patient from the bed. 환자를 천천히 침대에서 일으키세요.

년 월 일

1 Corinthians 1 : 21~24

21 For since in the
wisdom of God the world through its
wisdom did not know him, God was
pleased through the foolishness of what
was preached to save those who be-
lieve. 22 Jews demand signs and Greeks
look for wisdom, 23 but we preach Christ
crucified: a stumbling block to Jews and
foolishness to Gentiles, 24 but to those
whom God has called, both Jews and
Greeks, Christ the power of God and the
wisdom of God.

Ephesians 2 : 8~10

8 For it is by grace
you have been saved, through faith—and
this is not from yourselves, it is the gift
of God— 9 not by works, so that no one

look for 찾다
I will look for him as far as in me lies. 나는 내 힘이 미치는 한 그를 찾을 것이다.

년 월 일

can boast. 10 For we are God's hand-
work, created in Christ Jesus to do good
works, which God prepared in advance
for us to do.

Hebrews 11 : 5~6 5 By faith Enoch
was taken from this life, so that he did
not experience death; "He could not be
found, because God had taken him
away. For before he was taken, he was
commended as one who pleased God.
6 And without faith it is impossible to
please God, because anyone who
comes to him must believe that he ex-
ists and that he rewards those who
earnestly seek him.

James 2 : 15~17 15 Suppose a brother

take from …를 줄이다
How long will it take from here? 여기서부터 얼마나 걸리니?

or a sister is without clothes and daily
food. 16 If one of you says to them, "Go, in
peace; keep warm and well fed," but does
nothing about their physical needs, what
good is it? 17 In the same way, faith by it-
self, if it is not accompanied by action, is
dead.

James 2 : 23~26

23 And the scripture
was fulfilled that says, "Abraham be-
lieved God, and it was credited to him as
righteousness," and he was called God's
friend. 24 You see that a person is consid-
ered righteous by what they do and not
by faith alone. 25 In the same way, was
not even Rahab the prostitute consid-
ered righteous for what she did when

be accompanied by …을 동반하다
He was accompanied by his family. 그는 가족을 동반했다.

년 월 일

she gave lodging to the spies and sent
them off in a different direction? 26 As
the body without the spirit is dead, so
faith without deeds is dead.

1 Peter 1 : 7~9

7 These have come
so that the proven genuineness of your
faith—of greater worth than gold, which
perishes even though refined by
fire—may result in praise, glory and
honor when Jesus Christ is revealed.
8 Though you have not seen him, you
love him; and even though you do not
see him now, you believe in him and are
filled with an inexpressible and glorious
joy, 9 for you are receiving the end result
of your faith, the salvation of your souls.

send off …를 퇴장시키다
I will send you off to the airport. 내가 너를 공항까지 배웅할게.

년 월 일

1 John 5 : 10~12 10 Whoever believes
in the Son of God accepts this testimony.
Whoever does not believe God has
made him out to be a liar, because they
have not believed the testimony God
has given about his Son. 11 And this is the
testimony: God has given us eternal life,
and this life is in his Son. 12 Whoever has
the Son has life; whoever does not have
the Son of God does not have life.

Revelation 14 : 12 12 This calls for pa-
tient endurance on the part of the peo-
ple of God who keep his commands and
remain faithful to Jesus.

make out …을 알아보다
I don't make out what you say. 말씀하시는 게 무슨 말인지 모르겠어요.

년 월 일

I will bless them.

Numbers 6 : 24~27

24 "The LORD bless
you and keep you; 25 the LORD make his
face shine on you and be gracious to
you; 26 the LORD turn his face toward
you and give you peace." 27 "So they will
put my name on the Israelites, and I will
bless them."

Genesis 5 : 1~2

1 This is the written
account of Adam's family line. When God
created mankind, he made them in the
likeness of God. 2 He created them male
and female and blessed them. And he
named them "Mankind." when they

put on …을 입다
He put on a hat. 그는 모자를 뒤집어썼다.

년 월 일

were created.

Genesis 9 : 1~3

1 Then God blessed
Noah and his sons, saying to them, "Be
fruitful and increase in number and fill
the earth. 2 The fear and dread of you
will fall on all the beasts of the earth, and
on all the birds in the sky, on every crea-
ture that moves along the ground, and
on all the fish in the sea; they are given
into your hands. 3 Everything that lives
and moves about will be food for you.
Just as I gave you the green plants, I now
give you everything.

Genesis 22 : 16~18

16 and said, "I swear
by myself, declares the LORD, that be-
cause you have done this and have not

just as 꼭 …처럼
It is just as you say. 정말 네가 말하는 그대로다.

withheld your son, your only son, 17 I will
surely bless you and make your descen-
dants as numerous as the stars in the sky
and as the sand on the seashore. Your
descendants will take possession of the
cities of their enemies, 18 and through
your offspring all nations on earth will be
blessed, because you have obeyed me."

Deuteronomy 28 : 1~6

1 If you fully obey
the LORD your God and carefully follow
all his commands I give you today, the
LORD your God will set you high above
all the nations on earth. 2 All these bless-
ings will come on you and accompany
you if you obey the LORD your God: 3 You
will be blessed in the city and blessed in

as ~ as …만큼
He can do as much as you. 그도 너만큼이나 할 수 있다.

the country. 4 The fruit of your womb will
be blessed, and the crops of your land
and the young of your livestock—the
calves of your herds and the lambs of
your flocks. 5 Your basket and your knead-
ing trough will be blessed. 6 You will be
blessed when you come in and blessed
when you go out.

Psalms 1 : 1~6 1 Blessed is the one
who does not walk in step with the
wicked or stand in the way that sinners
take or sit in the company of mockers, 2 but
whose delight is in the law of the LORD,
and who meditates on his law day and
night. 3 That person is like a tree planted
by streams of water, which yields its fruit

be in step with 보조가 맞다
I couldn't be in step with her. 나는 그녀와 보조를 맞출 수 없었다.

in season and whose leaf does not
wither—whatever they do prospers. 4 Not
so the wicked! They are like chaff that
the wind blows away. 5 Therefore the
wicked will not stand in the judgment,
nor sinners in the assembly of the right-
eous. 6 For the LORD watches over the
way of the righteous, but the way of the
wicked leads to destruction.

Proverbs 3 : 13~20

13 Blessed are those
who find wisdom, those who gain un-
derstanding, 14 for she is more profitable
than silver and yields better returns than
gold. 15 She is more precious than rubies;
nothing you desire can compare with
her. 16 Long life is in her right hand; in her

compare with …과 비교가 되다
Don't compare yourself with those around you. 자신을 주위 사람들과 비교하지 마세요.

년 월 일

left hand are riches and honor. 17 Her
ways are pleasant ways, and all her paths
are peace. 18 She is a tree of life to those
who take hold of her; those who hold
her fast will be blessed. 19 By wisdom the
LORD laid the earth's foundations, by un-
derstanding he set the heavens in place;
20 by his knowledge the watery depths were
divided, and the clouds let drop the dew.

Malachi 3 : 10~12

10 Bring the whole
tithe into the storehouse, that there may
be food in my house. Test me in this,"
says the LORD Almighty, "and see if I will
not throw open the floodgates of
heaven and pour out so much blessing
that there will not be room enough to

take hold of …을 잡다
Be sure to take hold of it as tight as you can. 그것을 되도록 단단히 붙잡고 있어라.

store it. 11 I will prevent pests from de-
vouring your crops, and the vines in your
fields will not drop their fruit before it is
ripe," says the LORD Almighty. 12 "Then
all the nations will call you blessed, for
yours will be a delightful land," says the
LORD Almighty.

Matthew 5 : 3~12 3 "Blessed are the
poor in spirit, for theirs is the kingdom of
heaven. 4 Blessed are those who mourn,
for they will be comforted. 5 Blessed are
the meek, for they will inherit the earth.
6 Blessed are those who hunger and
thirst for righteousness, for they will be
filled. 7 Blessed are the merciful, for they
will be shown mercy. 8 Blessed are the

prevent from …을 막다
Nothing shall prevent me from doing my duty. 여하한 일이 있더라도 내 할 일은 한다.

pure in heart, for they will see God.
9 Blessed are the peacemakers, for they
will be called children of God. 10 Blessed
are those who are persecuted because
of righteousness, for theirs is the king-
dom of heaven. 11 "Blessed are you when
people insult you, persecute you and
falsely say all kinds of evil against you
because of me. 12 Rejoice and be glad,
because great is your reward in heaven,
for in the same way they persecuted the
prophets who were before you.

You may be careful to do everything written in it.

in the same way 같은 방법으로
You and your brother act in the same way. 너와 네 형은 똑같이 행동해.

Joshua 1 : 8~9
8 Keep this Book of
the Law always on your lips; meditate on
it day and night, so that you may be
careful to do everything written in it.
Then you will be prosperous and suc-
cessful. 9 Have I not commanded you?
Be strong and courageous. Do not be
afraid; do not be discouraged, for the
LORD your God will be with you wher-
ever you go."

Exodus 12 : 13~14
13 The blood will be
a sign for you on the houses where you
are; and when I see the blood, I will pass
over you. No destructive plague will
touch you when I strike Egypt. 14 "This is
a day you are to commemorate; for the

meditate on …에 관해서 명상하다
She meditated on the day's events. 그녀는 그날 일어난 일들을 되새겨 보았다.

년 월 일

generations to come you shall celebrate
it as a festival to the LORD—a lasting or-
dinance.

Exodus 15 : 26

26 He said, "If you lis-
ten carefully to the LORD your God and
do what is right in his eyes, if you pay at-
tention to his commands and keep all
his decrees, I will not bring on you any of
the diseases I brought on the Egyptians,
for I am the LORD, who heals you."

Exodus 19 : 5~6

5 Now if you obey
me fully and keep my covenant, then out
of all nations you will be my treasured
possession. Although the whole earth is
mine, 6 you will be for me a kingdom of
priests and a holy nation.' These are the

pay attention to …에 주목하다
I try not to pay attention to rumors. 나는 소문에는 신경 쓰지 않으려고 해요.

words you are to speak to the Israelites."

Exodus 20 : 1~17 1 And God spoke all
these words: 2 "I am the LORD your God,
who brought you out of Egypt, out of
the land of slavery. 3 "You shall have no
other gods before me. 4 "You shall not
make for yourself an image in the form
of anything in heaven above or on the
earth beneath or in the waters below. 5 You
shall not bow down to them or worship
them; for I, the LORD your God, am a jeal-
ous God, punishing the children for the
sin of the parents to the third and fourth
generation of those who hate me, 6 but
showing love to a thousand generations
of those who love me and keep my com-

bring ~ out …을 끌어내다
I brought her out of there. 나는 그녀를 거기서 데리고 나왔다.

년 월 일

mandments. 7 "You shall not misuse the
name of the LORD your God, for the
LORD will not hold anyone guiltless who
misuses his name. 8 "Remember the
Sabbath day by keeping it holy. 9 Six
days you shall labor and do all your
work, 10 but the seventh day is a sabbath
to the LORD your God. On it you shall not
do any work, neither you, nor your son
or daughter, nor your male or female ser-
vant, nor your animals, nor any foreigner
residing in your towns. 11 For in six days
the LORD made the heavens and the
earth, the sea, and all that is in them, but
he rested on the seventh day. Therefore
the LORD blessed the Sabbath day and

on it 최고로

He did it on it. 그는 그걸 최고로 해냈다.

made it holy. 12 "Honor your father and
your mother, so that you may live long
in the land the LORD your God is giving
you. 13 "You shall not murder. 14 "You
shall not commit adultery. 15 "You shall
not steal. 16 "You shall not give false tes-
timony against your neighbor. 17 "You
shall not covet your neighbor's house.
You shall not covet your neighbor's wife,
or his male or female servant, his ox or
donkey, or anything that belongs to your
neighbor."

Deuteronomy 6 : 1~3

1 These are the com-
mands, decrees and laws the LORD your
God directed me to teach you to ob-
serve in the land that you are crossing

belong to …에 속하다
Do you belong to any clubs? 당신은 동아리에 가입한 거 있나요?

년 월 일

the Jordan to possess, 2 so that you, your
children and their children after them
may fear the LORD your God as long as
you live by keeping all his decrees and
commands that I give you, and so that
you may enjoy long life. 3 Hear, Israel,
and be careful to obey so that it may go
well with you and that you may increase
greatly in a land flowing with milk and
honey, just as the LORD, the God of your
ancestors, promised you.

Proverbs 3 : 1~10

1 My son, do not
forget my teaching, but keep my com-
mands in your heart, 2 for they will pro-
long your life many years and bring you
peace and prosperity. 3 Let love and

so that …하도록 …하다
My heart beats so that I can hardly speak. 가슴이 마구 뛰어 거의 말을 할 수가 없다.

년 월 일

faithfulness never leave you; bind them
around your neck, write them on the
tablet of your heart. 4 Then you will win
favor and a good name in the sight of
God and man. 5 Trust in the LORD with
all your heart and lean not on your own
understanding; 6 in all your ways submit
to him, and he will make your paths
straight. 7 Do not be wise in your own
eyes; fear the LORD and shun evil. 8 This
will bring health to your body and nour-
ishment to your bones. 9 Honor the LORD
with your wealth, with the firstfruits of all
your crops; 10 then your barns will be
filled to overflowing, and your vats will
brim over with new wine.

in the sight of …가 보기에는
I live in sight of the school. 나는 학교가 보이는 곳에 산다.

년 월 일

Matthew 5 : 17~20

17 "Do not think
that I have come to abolish the Law or
the Prophets; I have not come to abolish
them but to fulfill them. 18 For truly I tell
you, until heaven and earth disappear,
not the smallest letter, not the least
stroke of a pen, will by any means disap-
pear from the Law until everything is ac-
complished. 19 Therefore anyone who
sets aside one of the least of these com-
mands and teaches others accordingly
will be called least in the kingdom of
heaven, but whoever practices and
teaches these commands will be called
great in the kingdom of heaven. 20 For I
tell you that unless your righteousness

set aside 곁에 두다
Both sides agreed to set aside the problem. 양측은 그 문제는 제쳐 두기로 했다.

surpasses that of the Pharisees and the
teachers of the law, you will certainly not
enter the kingdom of heaven.

Matthew 7 : 24~27

24 "Therefore every-
one who hears these words of mine and
puts them into practice is like a wise man
who built his house on the rock. 25 The
rain came down, the streams rose, and
the winds blew and beat against that
house; yet it did not fall, because it had
its foundation on the rock. 26 But every-
one who hears these words of mine and
does not put them into practice is like a
foolish man who built his house on sand.
27 The rain came down, the streams rose,
and the winds blew and beat against

come down 무너져 내리다
The roof come down during the night. 밤사이에 지붕이 내려앉았다.

that house, and it fell with a great crash."

Matthew 28 : 18~20

18 Then Jesus came
to them and said, "All authority in
heaven and on earth has been given to
me. 19 Therefore go and make disciples
of all nations, baptizing them in the
name of the Father and of the Son and
of the Holy Spirit, 20 and teaching them
to obey everything I have commanded
you. And surely I am with you always, to
the very end of the age."

Mark 4 : 14~20

14 The farmer sows
the word. 15 Some people are like seed
along the path, where the word is sown.
As soon as they hear it, Satan comes and
takes away the word that was sown in

as soon as …하자마자
As soon as I know the result, I'll let you know. 결과를 아는 대로 알려 드리겠습니다.

them. 16 Others, like seed sown on rocky
places, hear the word and at once re-
ceive it with joy. 17 But since they have
no root, they last only a short time. When
trouble or persecution comes because
of the word, they quickly fall away. 18 Still
others, like seed sown among thorns,
hear the word; 19 but the worries of this
life, the deceitfulness of wealth and the
desires for other things come in and
choke the word, making it unfruitful.
20 Others, like seed sown on good soil,
hear the word, accept it, and produce a
crop—some thirty, some sixty or some a
hundred times what was sown."

John 15 : 10~11

10 If you keep my

fall away 서서히 줄어들다
His friends fell away from him. 그의 친구들이 그로부터 떠났다.

commands, you will remain in my love,
just as I have kept my Father's com-
mands and remain in his love. 11 I have
told you this so that my joy may be in
you and that your joy may be complete.

Romans 2 : 12~13
12 All who sin apart
from the law will also perish apart from
the law, and all who sin under the law
will be judged by the law. 13 For it is not
those who hear the law who are right-
eous in God's sight, but it is those who
obey the law who will be declared right-
eous.

1 Corinthians 15 : 1~2
1 Now, brothers
and sisters, I want to remind you of the
gospel I preached to you, which you re-

apart from …외에는
He became serious apart from joking. 그는 농담을 그만 두더니 심각해졌다.

ceived and on which you have taken
your stand. 2 By this gospel you are
saved, if you hold firmly to the word I
preached to you. Otherwise, you have
believed in vain.

1 John 2 : 3~6
3 We know that we
have come to know him if we keep his
commands. 4 Whoever says, "I know
him," but does not do what he com-
mands is a liar, and the truth is not in that
person. 5 But if anyone obeys his word,
love for God is truly made complete in
them. This is how we know we are in
him: 6 Whoever claims to live in him
must live as Jesus did.

Revelation 1 : 1~3
1 The revelation from

in vain 허사가 되어
All his efforts ended in vain. 그의 공력도 마침내 허사였다.

년 월 일

Jesus Christ, which God gave him to
show his servants what must soon take
place. He made it known by sending his
angel to his servant John, 2 who testifies
to everything he saw—that is, the word
of God and the testimony of Jesus Christ.
3 Blessed is the one who reads aloud the
words of this prophecy, and blessed are
those who hear it and take to heart what
is written in it, because the time is near.

Revelation 22 : 18~21

18 I warn everyone
who hears the words of the prophecy of
this scroll: If anyone adds anything to
them, God will add to that person the
plagues described in this scroll. 19 And if
anyone takes words away from this scroll

add to …에 더하다
Is there anything else you want to add to that? 추가로 하실 말씀은 없으세요?

년 월 일

of prophecy, God will take away from
that person any share in the tree of life
and in the Holy City, which are described
in this scroll. 20 He who testifies to these
things says, "Yes, I am coming soon."
Amen. Come, Lord Jesus. 21 The grace of
the Lord Jesus be with God's people.
Amen.

Guide them on their way.

Exodus 13 : 21~22

21 By day the LORD
went ahead of them in a pillar of cloud
to guide them on their way and by night
in a pillar of fire to give them light, so

share in …을 서로 나누다
I have no share in the matter. 나는 그 일에 관계가 없다.

년 월 일

that they could travel by day or night.
22 Neither the pillar of cloud by day nor
the pillar of fire by night left its place in
front of the people.

Psalms 23 : 1~6

1 The LORD is my
shepherd, I lack nothing. 2 He makes me
lie down in green pastures, he leads me
beside quiet waters, 3 he refreshes my
soul. He guides me along the right paths
for his name's sake. 4 Even though I walk
through the darkest valley, I will fear no
evil, for you are with me; your rod and
your staff, they comfort me. 5 You pre-
pare a table before me in the presence
of my enemies. You anoint my head with
oil; my cup overflows. 6 Surely your good-

in the presence of …가 있는 데서
He was scolded in the presence of people. 그는 사람들 면전에서 책망당했다.

ness and love will follow me all the days
of my life, and I will dwell in the house of
the LORD forever.

John 10 : 14~16

14 "I am the good
shepherd; I know my sheep and my
sheep know me— 15 just as the Father
knows me and I know the Father—and I
lay down my life for the sheep. 16 I have
other sheep that are not of this sheep
pen. I must bring them also. They too will
listen to my voice, and there shall be one
flock and one shepherd.

Revelation 14 : 4~5

4 These are those
who did not defile themselves with
women, for they remained virgins. They
follow the Lamb wherever he goes. They

dwell in 살다
They dwelt in the middle of the forest. 그들은 숲 한가운데에 살았다.

were purchased from among mankind
and offered as firstfruits to God and the
Lamb. 5 No lie was found in their mouths;
they are blameless.

The LORD watches over you.

Psalms 121 : 1~8 1 I lift up my eyes to
the mountains—where does my help
come from? 2 My help comes from the
LORD, the Maker of heaven and earth.
3 He will not let your foot slip—he who
watches over you will not slumber; 4 in-
deed, he who watches over Israel will
neither slumber nor sleep. 5 The LORD

purchase from …에서 구입하다
The man is making a purchase from a newsstand. 남자가 신문 가판대에서 물건을 사고 있다.

년 월 일

watches over you—the LORD is your
shade at your right hand; 6 the sun will
not harm you by day, nor the moon by
night. 7 The LORD will keep you from all
harm—he will watch over your life; 8 the
LORD will watch over your coming and
going both now and forevermore.

Psalms 16 : 5~11

5 LORD, you alone
are my portion and my cup; you make
my lot secure. 6 The boundary lines have
fallen for me in pleasant places; surely I
have a delightful inheritance. 7 I will
praise the LORD, who counsels me; even
at night my heart instructs me. 8 I keep
my eyes always on the LORD. With him
at my right hand, I will not be shaken.

keep from …하지 못하게 하다
I could hardly keep from tears. 나는 눈물을 참을 수 없었다.

년 월 일

9 Therefore my heart is glad and my
tongue rejoices; my body also will rest
secure, 10 because you will not abandon
me to the realm of the dead, nor will you
let your faithful one see decay. 11 You
make known to me the path of life; you
will fill me with joy in your presence,
with eternal pleasures at your right
hand.

I will answer him.

Psalms 91 : 14~16

14 "Because he loves
me," says the LORD, "I will rescue him; I
will protect him, for he acknowledges

abandon oneself to …에 빠지다
She abandoned herself to animations recently. 그녀는 최근에 애니메이션에 빠졌다.

my name. 15 He will call on me, and I will
answer him; I will be with him in trouble,
I will deliver him and honor him. 16 With
long life I will satisfy him and show him
my salvation."

Psalms 37 : 4~6

4 Take Delight in
the LORD, and he will give you the de-
sires of your heart. 5 Commit your way
to the LORD; trust in him and he will do
this: 6 He will make your righteous re-
ward shine like the dawn, your vindica-
tion like the noonday sun.

Psalms 50 : 14~15

14 "Sacrifice thank
offerings to God, fulfill your vows to the
Most High, 15 and call on me in the day
of trouble; I will deliver you, and you will

call on 요청하다
If you need my hand, call on me any time. 내 도움이 필요하면 언제든지 연락해.

년 월 일

honor me."

Psalms 145 : 18~20

18 The LORD is near
to all who call on him, to all who call on
him in truth.
19 He fulfills the desires of
those who fear him; he hears their cry
and saves them.
20 The LORD watches
over all who love him, but all the wicked
he will destroy.

Isaiah 30 : 18~19

18 Yet the LORD
longs to be gracious to you; therefore he
will rise up to show you compassion. For
the LORD is a God of justice. Blessed are
all who wait for him!
19 People of Zion,
who live in Jerusalem, you will weep no
more. How gracious he will be when you
cry for help! As soon as he hears, he will

wait for …를 기다리다
Why didn't they wait for us? 왜 그 사람들은 우리를 기다리지 않았지?

answer you.

Jeremiah 33 : 2~3

2 "This is what the
LORD says, he who made the earth, the
LORD who formed it and established
it—the LORD is his name: 3 'Call to me
and I will answer you and tell you great
and unsearchable things you do not
know.'

Matthew 6 : 9~13

9 "This, then, is how
you should pray: " 'Our Father in heaven,
hallowed be your name, 10 your king-
dom come, your will be done, on earth
as it is in heaven. 11 Give us today our
daily bread. 12 And forgive us our debts,
as we also have forgiven our debtors.
13 And lead us not into temptation, but

be done 끝나다
Much yet remains to be done. 지금도 해야 할 일이 많다.

년 월 일

deliver us from the evil one.(for yours is
the kingdom and the power and the
glory forever. Amen.)'

Mark 11 : 22~24
22 "Have faith in
God," Jesus answered. 23 "Truly I tell you,
if anyone says to this mountain, 'Go,
throw yourself into the sea,' and does
not doubt in their heart but believes that
what they says will happen, it will be
done for them. 24 Therefore I tell you,
whatever you ask for in prayer, believe
that you have received it, and it will be
yours.

John 14 : 12~14
12 Very truly I tell
you, whoever believes in me will do the
works I have been doing, and they will

ask for …을 찾아오다
Let's learn how to ask for help! 도움을 요청하는 방법을 배워보아요!

do even greater things than these, be-
cause I am going to the Father. 13 And I
will do whatever you ask in my name, so
that the Father may be glorified in the
Son. 14 You may ask me for anything in
my name, and I will do it.

John 16 : 23~24
23 In that day you
will no longer ask me anything. Very
truly I tell you, my Father will give you
whatever you ask in my name. 24 Until
now you have not asked for anything in
my name. Ask and you will receive, and
your joy will be complete.

Philippians 4 : 6~7
6 Do not be anxious
about anything, but in every situation,
by prayer and petition, with thanksgiv-

be anxious about 속을 태우다
His family has been anxious about his health. 그의 가족은 그의 건강에 대해 염려해 왔다.

년 월 일

ing, present your requests to God. 7 And
the peace of God, which transcends all
understanding, will guard your hearts
and your minds in Christ Jesus.

1 Thessalonians 5 : 16~18

16 Rejoice always;
17 pray continually; 18 give thanks in all
circumstances; for this is God's will for
you in Christ Jesus.

1 Timothy 4 : 4~5

4 For everything
God created is good, and nothing is to
be rejected if it is received with thanks-
giving, 5 because it is consecrated by the
word of God and prayer.

James 1 : 2~5

2 Consider it pure
joy, my brothers and sisters, whenever
you face trials of many kinds, 3 because

receive with 받아들이다.
The people received with open arms. 사람들은 매우 환대해 주었다.

년 월 일

you know that the testing of your faith
produces perseverance. 4 Let persever-
ance finish its work so that you may be
mature and complete, not lacking any-
thing. 5 If any of you lacks wisdom, you
should ask God, who gives generously to
all without finding fault, and it will be
given to you.

1 John 5 : 13~15

13 I write these things
to you who believe in the name of the
Son of God so that you may know that
you have eternal life. 14 This is the confi-
dence we have in approaching God: that
if we ask anything according to his will,
he hears us. 15 And if we know that he
hears us—whatever we ask—we know

according to 따르면
Just do it according to the plan. 계획에 따라서만 행동해라.

년 월 일

that we have what we asked of him.

Good fruit.

Matthew 7 : 17~20 17 Likewise, every
good tree bears good fruit, but a bad
tree bears bad fruit. 18 A good tree can-
not bear bad fruit, and a bad tree cannot
bear good fruit. 19 Every tree that does
not bear good fruit is cut down and
thrown into the fire. 20 Thus, by their fruit
you will recognize them.

Genesis 2 : 15~17 15 The LORD God
took the man and put him in the Garden
of Eden to work it and take care of it.

throw into (어떤 상태에) 빠뜨리다
Bill was thrown into ecstasies over her. 빌은 그녀에게 정신이 팔렸다.

16 And the LORD God commanded the
man, "You are free to eat from any tree
in the garden; 17 but you must not eat
from the tree of the knowledge of good
and evil, for when you eat from it you will
certainly die."

John 15 : 1~8

1 "I am the true vine,
and my Father is the gardener. 2 He cuts
off every branch in me that bears no
fruit, while every branch that does bear
fruit he prunes so that it will be even
more fruitful. 3 You are already clean be-
cause of the word I have spoken to you.
4 Remain in me, as I also remain in you.
No branch can bear fruit by itself; it must
remain in the vine. Neither can you bear

free to 자유롭게 …하다
All members are free to use the reading room. 회원은 누구나 독서실을 사용할 수 있다.

년 월 일

fruit unless you remain in me.
5 "I am the
vine; you are the branches. If you remain
in me and I in you, you will bear much
fruit; apart from me you can do nothing.
6 If you do not remain in me, you are like
a branch that is thrown away and with-
ers; such branches are picked up, thrown
into the fire and burned.
7 If you remain
in me and my words remain in you, ask
whatever you wish, and it will be done
for you.
8 This is to my Father's glory, that
you bear much fruit, showing yourselves
to be my disciples.

1 Corinthians 14 : 12~15

12 So it is with you.
Since you are eager for gifts of the Spirit,
try to excel in those that build up the

excel in …에서 뛰어나다
I tried to excel in my studies. 나는 학업에 앞서려고 노력했다.

church. 13 For this reason the one who
speaks in a tongue should pray that they
may interpret what they say. 14 For if I
pray in a tongue, my spirit prays, but my
mind is unfruitful. 15 So what shall I do? I
will pray with my spirit, but I will also
pray with my understanding; I will sing
with my spirit, but I will also sing with my
understanding.

Galatians 5 : 22~23 22 But the fruit of
the Spirit is love, joy, peace, forbearance,
kindness, goodness, faithfulness, 23 gen-
tleness and self-control. Against such
things there is no law.

Ephesians 5 : 8~9 8 For you were once
darkness, but now you are light in the

the fruit of …의 결실
Wealth is the fruit of labor. 부는 노동의 산물이다.

년 월 일

Lord. Live as children of light 9 (for the
fruit of the light consists in all goodness,
righteousness and truth)

James 3 : 17~18

17 But the wisdom
that comes from heaven is first of all
pure; then peace-loving, considerate,
submissive, full of mercy and good fruit,
impartial and sincere. 18 Peacemakers
who sow in peace reap a harvest of
righteousness.

2 Peter 1 : 5~11

5 For this very rea-
son, make every effort to add to your
faith goodness; and to goodness, knowl-
edge; 6 and to knowledge, self-control;
and to self-control, perseverance; and to
perseverance, godliness; 7 and to godli-

consist in …에 있다
Happiness consists in trying to do one's duty. 행복은 자기 본분을 다하는 데 있다.

ness, mutual affection; and to mutual af-
fection, love. 8 For if you possess these
qualities in increasing measure, they will
keep you from being ineffective and un-
productive in your knowledge of our
Lord Jesus Christ. 9 But whoever does
not have them is nearsighted and blind,
forgetting that they have been cleansed
from their past sins. 10 Therefore, my
brothers and sisters, make every effect
to confirm your calling and election. For
if you do these things, you will never
stumble, 11 and you will receive a rich
welcome into the eternal kingdom of
our Lord and Savior Jesus Christ.

Revelation 22 : 1~2

1 Then the angel

clean from …에서 닦아내다
Who will clean the house from now on? 누가 이제부터 집안을 청소할 것인가?

showed me the river of the water of life,
as clear as crystal, flowing from the
throne of God and of the Lamb 2 down
the middle of the great street of the city.
On each side of the river stood the tree
of life, bearing twelve crops of fruit,
yielding its fruit every month. And the
leaves of the tree are for the healing of
the nations.

To do the will of him who sent me.

John 6 : 38~40 38 For I have come
down from heaven not to do my will but
to do the will of him who sent me. 39 And

flow from …에서 흐르다
Where does this water flow from?이 물은 어디에서 흘러나오는 거죠?

this is the will of him who sent me, that I
shall lose none of all those he has given
me, but raise them up at the last day.
40 For
my Father's will is that everyone who
looks to the Son and believes in him
shall have eternal life, and I will raise
them up at the last day."

Matthew 7 : 21

21 "Not everyone who
says to me, 'Lord, Lord,' will enter the
kingdom of heaven, but only the one
who does the will of my Father who is in
heaven.

Matthew 12 : 49~50

49 Pointing to his
disciples, he said, "Here are my mother
and my brothers.
50 For whoever does
the will of my Father in heaven is my

in heaven 하늘에 계신
Maestro, rest in peace in heaven! 선생님, 천국에서 편히 쉬십시오!

년 월 일

brother and sister and mother."

Luke 22 : 42~43

42 "Father, if you are
willing, take this cup from me; yet not
my will, but yours be done." 43 An angel
from heaven appeared to him and
strengthened him.

All people to be saved.

1 Timothy 2 : 3~6

3 This is good, and
pleases God our Savior, 4 who wants all
people to be saved and to come to a
knowledge of the truth. 5 For there is
one God and one mediator between
God and mankind, the man Christ Jesus,

appear to …에게 나타나다
He doesn't appear to be nervous at all. 그는 전혀 초조한 기색이 없다.

6 who gave himself as a ransom for all
people. This has now been witnessed to
at the proper time.

Matthew 19 : 25~26

25 When the disci-
ples heard this, they were greatly aston-
ished and asked, "Who then can be
saved?" 26 Jesus looked at them and said,
"With man this is impossible, but with
God all things are possible."

Mark 8 : 34~35

34 Then he called
the crowd to him along with his disciples
and said: "Whoever wants to be my dis-
ciple must deny themselves and take up
their cross and follow me. 35 For whoever
wants to save their life will lose it, but
whoever loses their life for me and for

ransom for …의 몸값을 지불하다
He spent a king's ransom for his wedding. 그는 결혼식에 돈을 왕창 썼다.

년 월 일

the gospel will save it.

Mark 16 : 15~16 15 He said to them,
"Go into all the world and preach the
gospel to all creation. 16 Whoever be-
lieves and is baptized will be saved, but
whoever does not believe will be con-
demned.

Colossians 2 : 13~15 13 When you were
dead in your sins and in the uncircumci-
sion of your flesh, God made you alive
with Christ. He forgave us all our sins,
14 having canceled the charge of our
legal indebtedness, which stood against
us and condemned us; he has taken it
away, nailing it to the cross. 15 And hav-
ing disarmed the powers and authori-

alive with …으로 붐벼
The sugar is alive with ants. 설탕에 개미가 우글거린다.

년 월 일

ties, he made a public spectacle of them,
triumphing over them by the cross.

2 Timothy 3 : 14~17

14 But as for you,
continue in what you have learned and
have become convinced of, because you
know those from whom you learned it,
15 and how from infancy you have known
the Holy Scriptures, which are able to
make you wise for salvation through
faith in Christ Jesus. 16 All Scripture is
God-breathed and is useful for teaching,
rebuking, correcting and training in
righteousness, 17 so that the servant of
God may be thoroughly equipped for
every good work.

equipped for …을 위해 준비된
He is well equipped for it. 그는 훌륭히 그 일을 할 수 있다.

년 월 일

God is love.

1 John 4 : 7~9

7 Dear friends, let us
love one another, for love comes from
God. Everyone who loves has been born
of God and knows God. 8 Whoever does
not love does not know God, because
God is love. 9 This is how God showed his
love among us: He sent his one and only
Son into the world that we might live
through him.

Mark 12 : 29~31

29 "The most impor-
tant one," answered Jesus, "is this: 'Hear,
O Israel: the Lord our God, the Lord is
one. 30 Love the Lord your God with all

one another 서로
The boys sit well with one another. 그 소년들은 서로 잘 어울린다.

your heart and with all your soul and
with all your mind and with all your
strength.' 31 The second is this: 'Love your
neighbor as yourself.' There is no com-
mandment greater than these."

Luke 11 : 42

42 "Woe to you Phar-
isees, because you give God a tenth of
your mint, rue and all other kinds of gar-
den herbs, but you neglect justice and
the love of God. You should have prac-
ticed the latter without leaving the for-
mer undone.

John 3 : 16~17

16 For God so loved
the world that he gave his one and only
Son, that whoever believes in him shall
not perish but have eternal life. 17 For

Woe to …에게 화가 미칠진저
She will bring woe to you. 그녀는 너에게 화를 가져올 것이다.

년 월 일

God did not send his Son into the world
to condemn the world, but to save the
world through him.

John 13 : 34~35

34 "A new command
I give you: Love one another. As I have
loved you, so you must love one another.
35 By this everyone will know that you are
my disciples, if you love one another."

Ephesians 4 : 11~15

11 So Christ himself
gave the apostles, the prophets, the
evangelists, the pastors and teachers,
12 to equip his people for works of serv-
ice, so that the body of Christ may be
built up 13 until we all reach unity in the
faith and in the knowledge of the Son of
God and become mature, attaining to

send into …에 내보내다
It will send him into bankrupt. 이 때문에 그는 파산할 것이다.

the whole measure of the fullness of
Christ. 14 Then we will no longer be in-
fants, tossed back and forth by the
waves, and blown here and there by
every wind of teaching and by the cun-
ning and craftiness of people in their de-
ceitful scheming. 15 Instead, speaking
the truth in love, we will grow to become
in every respect the mature body of him
who is the head, that is, Christ.

1 Peter 4 : 7~10

7 The end of all
things is near. Therefore be alert and of
sober mind so that you may pray. 8 Above
all, love each other deeply, because love
covers over a multitude of sins. 9 Offer
hospitality to one another without

above all 무엇보다도
Above all, he wants to live. 무엇보다도, 그는 살고 싶어한다.

grumbling. 10 Each of you should use
whatever gift you have received to serve
others, as faithful stewards of God's
grace in its various forms.

1 John 3 : 8~10

8 The one who does
what is sinful is of the devil, because the
devil has been sinning from the begin-
ning. The reason the Son of God ap-
peared was to destroy the devil's work.
9 No one who is born of God will con-
tinue to sin, because God's seed remains
in them; they cannot go on sinning, be-
cause they have been born of God. 10 This
is how we know who the children of God
are and who the children of the devil are:
Anyone who does not do what is right is

each of …의 각각
Each of you is very special. 여러분 각각은 매우 특별합니다.

not God's child, nor is anyone who does
not love their brother and sister.

1 John 5 : 1~4

1 Everyone who be-
lieves that Jesus is the Christ is born of
God, and everyone who loves the father
loves his child as well.
2 This is how we
know that we love the children of God:
by loving God and carrying out his com-
mands.
3 In fact, this is love for God: to
keep his commands. And his commands
are not burdensome,
4 for everyone
born of God overcomes the world. This
is the victory that has overcome the
world, even our faith.

as well 또한
Do you love singing as well? 노래 부르는 것도 좋아하십니까?

년 월 일

When the Holy Spirit comes on you.

Acts 1 : 8~9

8 But you will re-
ceive power when the Holy Spirit comes
on you; and you will be my witnesses in
Jerusalem, and in all Judea and Samaria,
and to the ends of the earth." 9 After he
said this, he was taken up before their
very eyes, and a cloud hid him from their
sight.

Ezekiel 36 : 26~28

26 I will give you a
new heart and put a new spirit in you; I
will remove from you your heart of stone
and give you a heart of flesh. 27 And I will
put my Spirit in you and move you to fol-

come on 등장하다
What time does the movie come on? 그 영화는 몇 시에 하니?

low my decrees and be careful to keep
my laws. 28 Then You will live in the land
I gave your ancestors; you will be my
people, and I will be your God.

Joel 2 : 28~30

28 "And afterward, I
will pour out my Spirit on all people. Your
sons and daughters will prophesy, your
old men will dream dreams, your young
men will see visions. 29 Even on my ser-
vants, both men and women, I will pour
out my Spirit in those days. 30 I will show
wonders in the heavens and on the
earth, blood and fire and billows of
smoke.

John 4 : 23~24

23 Yet a time is com-
ing and has now come when the true

pour out 쏟아져 나오다
Pour out water little by little. 물을 조금씩 쏟아라.

년 월 일

worshipers will worship the Father in the
Spirit and in truth, for they are the kind
of worshipers the Father seeks. 24 God is
spirit, and his worshipers must worship
in the Spirit and in truth."

John 16 : 13~15

13 But when he, the
Spirit of truth, comes, he will guide you
into all the truth. He will not speak on his
own; he will speak only what he hears,
and he will tell you what is yet to come.
14 He will glorify me because it is from me
that he will receive what he will make
known to you. 15 All that belongs to the
Father is mine. That is why I said the
Spirit will receive from me what he will
make known to you.

in truth 사실은
In truth, they are not interested. 사실, 그들은 관심이 없다.

년 월 일

Romans 8 : 14~15

14 For those who
are led by the Spirit of God are the chil-
dren of God. 15 The Spirit you received
does not make you slaves, so that you
live in fear again; rather, the Spirit you re-
ceived brought about your adoption to
sonship. And by him we cry, "Abba, Fa-
ther."

Romans 14 : 17~18

17 For the kingdom
of God is not a matter of eating and
drinking, but of righteousness, peace
and joy in the Holy Spirit, 18 because any-
one who serves Christ in this way is
pleasing to God and receives human ap-
proval.

1 Corinthians 2 : 10~12

10 these are the

bring about 야기하다
We hope to see you bring about changes. 당신을 통해 사람들이 변화되기를 바란다.

things God has revealed to us by his
Spirit. The Spirit searches all things, even
the deep things of God. 11 For who
knows a person's thoughts except their
own spirit within them? In the same way
no one knows the thoughts of God ex-
cept the Spirit of God. 12 What we have
received is not the spirit of the world, but
the Spirit who is from God, so that we
may understand what God has freely
given us.

1 Corinthians 6 : 19~20

19 Do you not know
that your bodies are temples of the Holy
Spirit, who is in you, whom you have re-
ceived from God? You are not your own;
20 you were bought at a price. Therefore

all things 모든 것
All things are won by industry. 모든 것은 근면에 의해서 얻어진다.

honor God with your bodies.

Galatians 6 : 6~8
6 Nevertheless, the
one who receives instruction in the word
should share all good things with their
instructor. 7 Do not be deceived: God
cannot be mocked. A man reaps what he
sows. 8 Whoever sows to please their
flesh, from the flesh will reap destruc-
tion; whoever sows to please the Spirit,
from the Spirit will reap eternal life.

It is finished.

John 19 : 28~30
28 Later, knowing
that everything had now been finished,

nevertheless 그럼에도 불구하고
Nevertheless, he couldn't deny the truth. 그럼에도 불구하고, 그는 진리를 부정할 수 없었다.

년 월 일

and so that Scripture would be fulfilled,
Jesus said, "I am thirsty." 29 A jar of wine
vinegar was there, so they soaked a
sponge in it, put the sponge on a stalk of
the hyssop plant, and lifted it to Jesus'
lips. 30 When he had received the drink,
Jesus said, "It is finished." With that, he
bowed his head and gave up his spirit.

Genesis 18 : 18~19

18 Abraham will
surely become a great and powerful na-
tion, and all nations on earth will be
blessed through him. 19 For I have cho-
sen him, so that he will direct his chil-
dren and his household after him to
keep the way of the LORD by doing what
is right and just, so that the LORD will

be fulfilled 이루어지다
The prophecy will be fulfilled soon. 그 예언은 곧 실현될 것이다.

bring about for Abraham what he has
promised him."

Exodus 2 : 24~25

24 God heard their
groaning and he remembered his
covenant with Abraham, with Isaac and
with Jacob. 25 So God looked on the Is-
raelites and was concerned about them.

Joshua 21 : 43~45

43 So the LORD gave
Israel all the land he had sworn to give
their ancestors, and they took posses-
sion of it and settled there. 44 The LORD
gave them rest on every side, just as he
had sworn to their ancestors. Not one of
their enemies withstood them; the LORD
gave all their enemies into them their
hands. 45 Not one of all the LORD's good

be concerned about …에 관심을 가지다
Who should I be concerned about? 누구를 가장 주의해야 하지?

년 월 일

promises to Israel failed; every one was
fulfilled.

Matthew 1 : 21~23

21 She will give birth
to a son, and you are to give him the
name Jesus, because he will save his
people from their sins." 22 All this took
place to fulfill what the Lord had said
through the prophet: 23 "The virgin will
conceive and give birth to a son, and
they will call him Immanuel"(which
means "God with us").

Matthew 24 : 35~36

35 Heaven and earth
will pass away, but my words will never
pass away. 36 "But about that day or hour
no one knows, not even the angels in
heaven, nor the Son, but only the Father.

pass away 없어지다
His illness will soon pass away. 그의 병은 곧 나을 것이다.

년 월 일

John 14 : 6

6 Jesus answered, "I
am the way and the truth and the life. No
one comes to the Father except through
me.

Romans 1 : 2~4

2 the gospel he
promised beforehand through his
prophets in the Holy Scriptures 3 regard-
ing his Son, who as to his earthly life was
a descendant of David, 4 and who through
the Spirit of holiness was appointed the
Son of God in power by his resurrection
from the dead: Jesus Christ our Lord.

1 Corinthians 15 : 3~8

3 For what I re-
ceived I passed on to you as of first im-
portance: that Christ died for our sins
according to the Scriptures, 4 that he

except through …외에는
I have nothing to say except through it. 나는 그것 외에는 할 말이 없다.

년 월 일

was buried, that he was raised on the
third day according to the Scriptures,
5 and that he appeared to Cephas, and
then to the Twelve. 6 After that, he ap-
peared to more than five hundred of the
brothers and sisters at the same time,
most of whom are still living, though
some have fallen asleep. 7 Then he ap-
peared to James, then to all the apostles,
8 and last of all he appeared to me also,
as to one abnormally born.

1 Corinthians 15 : 14~19 14 And if Christ has
not been raised, our preaching is useless
and so is your faith. 15 More than that, we
are then found to be false witnesses
about God, for we have testified about

more than that 그보다 더
I don't know much more than that. 그 이상은 저도 모릅니다.

God that he raised Christ from the dead.
But he did not raise him if in fact the
dead are not raised. 16 For if the dead are
not raised, then Christ has not been
raised either. 17 And if Christ has not
been raised, your faith is futile; you are
still in your sins. 18 Then those also who
have fallen asleep in Christ are lost. 19 If
only for this life we have hope in Christ,
we are of all people most to be pitied.

2 Corinthians 7 : 1 1 Therefore, since
we have these promises, dear friends, let
us purify ourselves from everything that
contaminates body and spirit, perfecting
holiness out of reverence for God.

Philippians 2 : 9~11 9 Therefore God ex-

fall asleep 잠들다
Kat has fallen asleep on the sofas. 캣은 소파에서 잠들었다.

년 월 일

alted him to the highest place and gave
him the name that is above every name,
10 that at the name of Jesus every knee
should bow, in heaven and on earth and
under the earth, 11 and every tongue ac-
knowledge that Jesus Christ is Lord, to
the glory of God the Father.

Hebrews 1 : 1~3

1 In the past God
spoke to our ancestors through the
prophets at many times and in various
ways, 2 but in these last days he has spo-
ken to us by his Son, whom he ap-
pointed heir of all things, and through
whom also he made the universe. 3 The
Son is the radiance of God's glory and
the exact representation of his being,

in the past 이전에
In the past doctors didn't know why. 과거엔 의사들이 왜 그런지를 몰랐었다.

sustaining all things by his powerful
word. After he had provided purification
for sins, he sat down at the right hand of
the Majesty in heaven.

2 Peter 1 : 3~4

3 His divine power
has given us everything we need for a
godly life through our knowledge of him
who called us by his own glory and
goodness. 4 Through these he has given
us his very great and precious promises,
so that through them you may partici-
pate in the divine nature, having es-
caped the corruption in the world
caused by evil desires.

2 Peter 3 : 8~14

8 But do not forget
this one thing, dear friends: With the

provide for …을 부양하다
I must provide for my family. 나는 가족을 먹여 살려야만 한다.

년 월 일

Lord a day is like a thousand years, and
a thousand years are like a day. 9 The
Lord is not slow in keeping his promise,
as some understand slowness. Instead
he is patient with you, not wanting any-
one to perish, but everyone to come to
repentance. 10 But the day of the Lord
will come like a thief. The heavens will
disappear with a roar; the elements will
be destroyed by fire, and the earth and
everything done in it will be laid bare.
11 Since everything will be destroyed in
this way, what kind of people ought you
to be? You ought to live holy and godly
lives 12 as you look forward to the day of
God and speed its coming. That day will

be destroyed by fire 소실되다
The house was altogether destroyed by fire. 그 집은 화재로 전부 소실되었다.

bring about the destruction of the heav-
ens by fire, and the elements will melt in
the heat. 13 But in keeping with his
promise we are looking forward to a
new heaven and a new earth, where
righteousness dwells. 14 So then, dear
friends, since you are looking forward to
this, make every effort to be found spot-
less, blameless and at peace with him.

We will be with the Lord forever.

1 Thessalonians 4 : 16~17 16 For the Lord him-
self will come down from heaven, with a
loud command, with the voice of the

in keeping with …와 일치하여
His actions are not in keeping with his promises. 그의 행동은 약속과 일치하지 않는다.

archangel and with the trumpet call of
God, and the dead in Christ will rise first.
17 After that, we who are still alive and are
left will be caught up together with
them in the clouds to meet the Lord in
the air. And so we will be with the Lord
forever.

Luke 20 : 34~36

34 Jesus replied,
"The people of this age marry and are
given in marriage. 35 But those who are
considered worthy of taking part in the
age to come and in the resurrection
from the dead will neither marry nor be
given in marriage, 36 and they can no
longer die; for they are like the angels.
They are God's children, since they are

after that 그 후
After that day, they asked for more money. 그날 이후 그들은 더 많은 돈을 요구했다.

children of the resurrection.

John 5 : 26~29

26 For as the Father
has life in himself, so he has granted the
Son also to have life in himself. 27 And he
has given him authority to judge be-
cause he is the Son of Man. 28 "Do not be
amazed at this, for a time is coming
when all who are in their graves will hear
his voice 29 and come out—those who
have done what is good will rise to live,
and those who have done what is evil
will rise to be condemned.

John 14 : 1~3

1 "Do not let your
hearts be troubled. You believe in God;
believe also in me. 2 My Father's house
has many rooms; if that were not so,

be amazed at …에 깜짝 놀라다
Some of you may be amazed at the results. 여러분 중 일부는 이 결과에 놀랄 수도 있다.

년 월 일

would I have told you that I am going
there to prepare a place for you? 3 And if
I go and prepare a place for you, I will
come back and take you to be with me
that you also may be where I am.

Romans 6 : 10~11

10 The death he
died, he died to sin once for all; but the
life he lives, he lives to God. 11 In the
same way, count yourselves dead to sin
but alive to God in Christ Jesus.

1 Corinthians 9 : 25~27

25 Everyone who
competes in the games goes into strict
training. They do it to get a crown that
will not last, but we do it to get a crown
that will last forever. 26 Therefore I do not
run like someone running aimlessly; I do

once for all 이번만
I say this once for all. 이 일은 분명히 말해둔다.

not fight like a boxer beating the air.
27 No, I strike a blow to my body and
make it my slave so that after I have
preached to others, I myself will not be
disqualified for the prize.

1 Corinthians 15 : 20~22
20 But Christ has in-
deed been raised from the dead, the first-
fruits of those who have fallen asleep.
21 For since death came through a man,
the resurrection of the dead comes also
through a man. 22 For as in Adam all die,
so in Christ all will be made alive.

Philippians 3 : 13~14
13 Brothers and sis-
ters, I do not consider myself yet to have
taken hold of it. But one thing I do: For-
getting what is behind and straining to-

be disqualified for 자격을 잃다
he was disqualified for a false start. 그는 부정출발로 실격처리 되었다.

년 월 일

ward what is ahead, 14 I press on toward
the goal to win the prize for which God
has called me heavenward in Christ Jesus.

Titus 2 : 12~14

12 It teaches us to
say "No" to ungodliness and worldly pas-
sions, and to live self-controlled, upright
and godly lives in this present age, 13 while
we wait for the blessed hope—the ap-
pearing of the glory our great God and
Savior, Jesus Christ, 14 who gave himself
for us to redeem us from all wickedness
and to purify for himself a people that
are his very own, eager to do what is
good.

Titus 3 : 4~7

4 But when the kind-
ness and love of God our Savior ap-

press on …을 누르다
Press on with your initial aim. 네 초기 목표를 강행해라.

년 월 일

peared, 5 he saved us, not because of
righteous things we had done, but be-
cause of his mercy. He saved us through
the washing of rebirth and renewal by
the Holy Spirit, 6 whom he poured out
on us generously through Jesus Christ
our Savior, 7 so that, having been justi-
fied by his grace, we might become heirs
having the hope of eternal life.

Hebrews 4 : 10~14 10 for anyone who
enters God's rest also rests from their
works, just as God did from his. 11 Let us,
therefore, make every effort to enter that
rest, so that no one will perish by follow-
ing their example of disobedience. 12 For
the word of God is alive and active.

example of 일례를 들면
This is an example of the power of language. 이것이 언어의 힘에 대한 하나의 예이다.

년 월 일

Sharper than any double-edged sword,
it penetrates even to dividing soul and
spirit, joints and marrow; it judges the
thoughts and attitudes of the heart.
13 Nothing in all creation is hidden from
God's sight. Everything is uncovered and
laid bare before the eyes of him to
whom we must give account. 14 There-
fore, since we have a great high priest
who has ascended into heaven, Jesus
the Son of God, let us hold firmly to the
faith we profess.

Hebrews 6 : 17~20

17 Because God
wanted to make the unchanging nature
of his purpose very clear to the heirs of
what was promised, he confirmed it with

hide from …에게 비밀로 하다
Is there anything you're trying to hide from him? 그에게 숨기고 싶은 것이 있니?

an oath. 18 God did this so that, by two
unchangeable things in which it is im-
possible for God to lie, we who have fled
to take hold of the hope set before us
may be greatly encouraged. 19 We have
this hope as an anchor for the soul, firm
and secure. It enters the inner sanctuary
behind the curtain, 20 where our forerun-
ner, Jesus, has entered on our behalf. He
has become a high priest forever, in the
order of Melchizedek.

Hebrews 9 : 27~28

27 Just as people are
destined to die once, and after that to
face judgment, 28 so Christ was sacrificed
once to take away the sins of many; and
he will appear a second time, not to bear

be destined to 운명 지어지다
They are destined never to meet again. 그들은 다시 만날 수 없는 운명이다.

년 월 일

sin, but to bring salvation to those who
are waiting for him.

1 Peter 1 : 2~4

2 who have been
chosen according to the foreknowledge
of God the Father, through the sanctify-
ing work of the Spirit, to be obedient to
Jesus Christ and sprinkled with his
blood: Grace and peace be yours in
abundance. 3 Praise be to the God and
Father of our Lord Jesus Christ! In his
great mercy he has given us new birth
into a living hope through the resurrec-
tion of Jesus Christ from the dead, 4 and
into an inheritance that can never perish,
spoil or fade. This inheritance is kept in
heaven for you,

in abundance 풍부하게
They lived in abundance. 그들은 풍족하게 살았다.

1 Peter 1 : 18~21 18 For you know
that it was not with perishable things
such as silver or gold that you were re-
deemed from the empty way of life
handed down to you from your ances-
tors, 19 but with the precious blood of
Christ, a lamb without blemish or defect.
20 He was chosen before the creation of
the world, but was revealed in these last
times for your sake. 21 Through him you
believe in God, who raised him from the
dead and glorified him, and so your faith
and hope are in God.

1 John 3 : 2~3 2 Dear friends, now
we are children of God, and what we will
be has not yet been made known. But

for your sake 너의 체면을 보아
I'm only doing it for your sake. 오로지 널 위해서 이걸 하고 있는 거야.

년 월 일

we know that when Christ appears, we
shall be like him, for we shall see him as
he is. 3 All who have this hope in him pu-
rify themselves, just as he is pure.

Revelation 10 : 5~7

5 Then the angel I
had seen standing on the sea and on the
land raised his right hand to heaven. 6 And
he swore by him who lives for ever and
ever, who created the heavens and all
that is in them, the earth and all that is
in it, and the sea and all that is in it, and
said, "There will be no more delay! 7 But
in the days when the seventh angel is
about to sound his trumpet, the mystery
of God will be accomplished, just as he
announced to his servants the prophets."

no more 그 이상 …하지 않다
It's really important there're no more delays. 더 이상 지연이 되지 않는 게 정말 중요해.

NIV개정

약속의 성경 영어 요절 따라쓰기

부록

원어민 발음 / 한글개역개정 수록

✦ 알파벳 대문자, 소문자, 발음기호와 발음

A a [eɪ] 에이	**B b** [biː] 비	**C c** [siː] 시	**D d** [diː] 디
E e [iː] 이	**F f** [ef] 에프	**G g** [dʒiː] 지	**H h** [eɪtʃ] 에이치
I i [aɪ] 아이	**J j** [dʒeɪ] 제이	**K k** [keɪ] 케이	**L l** [el] 엘
M m [em] 엠	**N n** [en] 엔	**O o** [oʊ] 오	**P p** [piː] 피
Q q [kjuː] 큐	**R r** [ɑː(r)] 아르	**S s** [es] 에스	**T t** [tiː] 티
U u [juː] 유	**V v** [viː] 브이	**W w** [ˈdʌbljuː] 더블유	**X x** [eks] 엑스
Y y [waɪ] 와이	**Z z** [zed/ziː] 지		

The righteous will live by faith. 오직 의인은 믿음으로 말미암아 살리라

Romans 1 : 16~17

16 For I am not ashamed of the gospel, because it is the power of God that brings salvation to everyone who believes: first to the Jew, then to the Gentile.
포어 아이 앰 낫 어셰임드 어브 더 가스펄, 비카즈 잇 이즈 더 파워 어브 가드 댓 브링즈 샐베이션 투 에브리원 후 빌리브즈 퍼스트 투 더 주, 덴 투 더 젠타일.
내가 복음을 부끄러워하지 아니하노니 이 복음은 모든 믿는 자에게 구원을 주시는 하나님의 능력이 됨이라 먼저는 유대인에게요 그리고 헬라인에게로다

17 For in the gospel the righteousness of God is revealed—a righteousness that is by faith from first to last, just as it is written: "The righteous will live by faith."
포어 인 더 가스펄 더 라이쳐스니스 어브 가드 이즈 리빌드 에이 라이쳐스니스 댓 이즈 바이 페이쓰 프럼 퍼스트 투 래스트, 저스트 애즈 잇 이즈 리턴 더 라이쳐스 윌 리브 바이 페이쓰.
복음에는 하나님의 의가 나타나서 믿음으로 믿음에 이르게 하나니 기록된 바 오직 의인은 믿음으로 말미암아 살리라 함과 같으니라

Mark 9 : 23~24

23 " 'If you can'?" said Jesus. "Everything is possible for one who believes."
이프 유 캔? 세드 지저스. 에브리씽 이즈 파서벌 포어 원 후 빌리브즈.
예수께서 이르시되 할 수 있거든이 무슨 말이냐 믿는 자에게는 능히 하지 못할 일이 없느니라 하시니

24 Immediately the boy's father exclaimed, "I do believe; help me overcome my unbelief!"
이미디엇리 더 보이즈 파더 익스클레임드, 아이 두 빌리브 헬프 미 오우버컴 마이 언빌리프!
곧 그 아이의 아버지가 소리를 질러 이르되 내가 믿나이다 나의 믿음 없는 것을 도와 주소서 하더라

Mark 16 : 17~20

17 And these signs will accompany those who believe: In my name they will drive out demons; they will speak in new tongues;
언드 디즈 사인즈 윌 어컴퍼니 도우즈 후 빌리브 인 마이 네임 데이 윌 드라이브 아웃 디먼즈 데이 윌 스픽 인 누 텅즈
믿는 자들에게는 이런 표적이 따르리니 곧 그들이 내 이름으로 귀신을 쫓아내며 새 방언을 말하며

18 they will pick up snakes with their hands; and when they drink deadly poison, it will not hurt them at all; they will place their hands on sick people, and they will get well."
데이 윌 픽 업 스네익스 윋 데어 핸즈 언드 웬 데이 드링크 데들리 포이전, 잇 윌 낫 허트 뎀 앳 올 데이 윌 플레이스 데어 핸즈 안 식 피펄, 언드 데이 윌 겟 웰.
뱀을 집어올리며 무슨 독을 마실지라도 해를 받지 아니하며 병든 사람에게 손을 얹은즉 나으리라 하시더라

19 After the Lord Jesus had spoken to them, he was taken up into heaven and he sat at the right hand of God.
애프터 더 로어드 지저스 해드 스포우컨 투 뎀, 히 와즈 테이컨 업 인투 헤번 언드 히 샛 앳 더 라이트 핸드 어브 갓.
주 예수께서 말씀을 마치신 후에 하늘로 올려지사 하나님 우편에 앉으시니라

20 Then the disciples went out and preached everywhere, and the Lord worked with them and confirmed his word by the signs that accompanied it.
덴 더 디사이펄즈 웬트 아웃 언드 프리치트 에브리웨어, 언드 더 로어드 워크트 윋 뎀 언드 컨펌드 히즈 워드 바이 더 사인즈 댓 어컴퍼니드 잇.
제자들이 나가 두루 전파할새 주께서 함께 역사하사 그 따르는 표적으로 말씀을 확실히 증언하시니라

John 1 : 12~13

12 Yet to all who did receive him, to those who believed in his name, he gave the right to become children of God—
옛 투 올 후 디드 러시브 힘, 투 도우즈 후 빌리브드 인 히즈 네임, 히 게이브 더 라이트 투 비컴 칠드런 어브 가드
영접하는 자 곧 그 이름을 믿는 자들에게는 하나님의 자녀가 되는 권세를 주셨으니

13 children born not of natural descent, nor of human decision or a husband's will, but born of God.

칠드런 본 낫 어브 내처럴 디센트, 노어 어브 휴먼 디시전 오어 어 허즈번즈 윌, 벗 본 어브 가드.
이는 혈통으로나 육정으로나 사람의 뜻으로 나지 아니하고 오직 하나님께로부터 난 자들이니라

John 3 : 16

16 For God so loved the world that he gave his one and only Son, that whoever believes in him shall not perish but have eternal life.
포어 가드 소우 러브드 더 월드 댓 히 게이브 히즈 원 언드 오운리 선, 댓 후에버 빌리브즈 인 힘 섈 낫 페어리쉬 벗 해브 이터널 라이프.
하나님이 세상을 이처럼 사랑하사 독생자를 주셨으니 이는 그를 믿는 자마다 멸망하지 않고 영생을 얻게 하려 하심이라

John 12 : 44~50

44 Then Jesus cried out, "Whoever believes in me does not believe in me only, but in the one who sent me.
덴 지저스 크라이드 아웃, 후에버 빌리브즈 인 미 더즈 낫 빌리브 인 미 오운리, 벗 인 더 원 후 센트 미.
예수께서 외쳐 이르시되 나를 믿는 자는 나를 믿는 것이 아니요 나를 보내신 이를 믿는 것이며

45 The one who looks at me is seeing the one who sent me.
더 원 후 룩스 앳 미 이즈 시잉 더 원 후 센트 미.
나를 보는 자는 나를 보내신 이를 보는 것이니라

46 I have come into the world as a light, so that no one who believes in me should stay in darkness.
아이 해브 컴 인투 더 월드 애즈 어 라이트, 소우 댓 노우 원 후 빌리브즈 인 미 슈드 스테이 인 다크네스.
나는 빛으로 세상에 왔나니 무릇 나를 믿는 자로 어둠에 거하지 않게 하려 함이로라

47 "If anyone hears my words but does not keep them, I do not judge that person. For I did not come to judge the world, but to save the world.
이프 에니원 히어즈 마이 워즈 벗 더즈 낫 킵 뎀, 아이 두 낫 저지 댓 퍼얼슨. 포어 아이 디드 낫 컴 투 저지 더 월드, 벗 투 세이브 더 월드.
사람이 내 말을 듣고 지키지 아니할지라도 내가 그를 심판하지 아니하노라 내가 온 것은 세상을 심판하려 함이 아니요 세상을 구원하려 함이로라

48 There is a judge for the one who rejects me and does not accept my words; the very words I have spoken will condemn them at the last day.
데어 이즈 어 저지 포어 더 원 후 리젝트스 미 언드 더즈 낫 억셉트 마이 워즈 더 베어리 워즈 아이 해브 스포우컨 윌 컨뎀 뎀 앳 더 래스트 데이.
나를 저버리고 내 말을 받지 아니하는 자를 심판할 이가 있으니 곧 내가 한 그 말이 마지막 날에 그를 심판하리라

49 For I did not speak on my own, but the Father who sent me commanded me to say all that I have spoken.
포어 아이 디드 낫 스픽 안 마이 오운, 벗 더 파더 후 센트 미 커맨디드 미 투 세이 올 댓 아이 해브 스포우컨.
내가 내 자의로 말한 것이 아니요 나를 보내신 아버지께서 내가 말할 것과 이를 것을 친히 명령하여 주셨으니

50 I know that his command leads to eternal life. So whatever I say is just what the Father has told me to say."
아이 노우 댓 히즈 커맨드 리즈 투 이터널 라이프. 소우 워테버 아이 세이 이즈 저스트 윗 더 파더 해즈 토울드 미 투 세이.
나는 그의 명령이 영생인 줄 아노라 그러므로 내가 이르는 것은 내 아버지께서 내게 말씀하신 그대로니라 하시니라

John 17 : 3~5

3 Now this is eternal life: that they know you, the only true God, and Jesus Christ, whom you have sent.
나우 디스 이즈 이터널 라이프 댓 데이 노우 유, 디 오운리 트루 가드, 언드 지저스 크라이스트, 훔 유 해브 센트.
영생은 곧 유일하신 참 하나님과 그가 보내신 자 예수 그리스도를 아는 것이니이다

4 I have brought you glory on earth by finishing the work you gave me to do.
아이 해브 브롯 유 글로어리 안 어쓰 바이 피니쉥 더 웍 유 게이브 미 투 두.
아버지께서 내게 하라고 주신 일을 내가 이루어 아버지를 이 세상에서 영화롭게 하였사오니

5 And now, Father, glorify me in your presence with the glory I had with you before the world began.
언드 나우, 파더, 글로어러파이 미 인 요어 프레전스 윋 더 글로어리 아이 해드 윋 유 비포어 더 월드 비갠.
아버지여 창세 전에 내가 아버지와 함께 가졌던 영화로써 지금도 아버지와 함께 나를 영화롭게 하옵소서

John 20 : 27~29

27 Then he said to Thomas, "Put your finger here; see my hands. Reach out your hand and put it into my side. Stop doubting and believe."
덴 히 세드 투 타머스, 풋 요어 핑거 히어 시 마이 핸즈. 리치 아웃 요어 핸드 언드 풋 잇 인투 마이 사이드. 스탑 다우팅 언드 빌리브.
도마에게 이르시되 네 손가락을 이리 내밀어 내 손을 보고 네 손을 내밀어 내 옆구리에 넣어 보라 그리하여 믿음 없는 자가 되지 말고 믿는 자가 되라

28 Thomas said to him, "My Lord and my God!"
타머스 세드 투 힘, 마이 로어드 언드 마이 가드!
도마가 대답하여 이르되 나의 주님이시요 나의 하나님이시니이다

29 Then Jesus told him, "Because you have seen me, you have believed; blessed are those who have not seen and yet have believed."
덴 지저스 토울드 힘, 비카즈 유 해브 신 미, 유 해브 빌리브드 블레스트 아아 도우즈 후 해브 낫 신 언드 옛 해브 빌리브드.
예수께서 이르시되 너는 나를 본 고로 믿느냐 보지 못하고 믿는 자들은 복되도다 하시니라

Romans 3 : 29~31

29 Or is God the God of Jews only? Is he not the God of Gentiles too? Yes, of Gentiles too,
오어 이즈 가드 더 가드 어브 주즈 오운리? 이즈 히 낫 더 가드 어브 젠타일즈 투? 예스, 어브 젠타일즈 투,
하나님은 다만 유대인의 하나님이시냐 또한 이방인의 하나님은 아니시냐 진실로 이방인의 하나님도 되시느니라

30 since there is only one God, who will justify the circumcised by faith and the uncircumcised through that same faith.
신스 데어 이즈 오운리 원 가드, 후 윌 저스터파이 더 서컴사이즈드 바이 페이쓰 언드 디 언서컴사이즈드 쓰루 댓 세임 페이쓰.
할례자도 믿음으로 말미암아 또한 무할례자도 믿음으로 말미암아 의롭다 하실 하나님은 한 분이시니라

31 Do we, then, nullify the law by this faith? Not at all! Rather, we uphold the law.
두 위, 덴, 널러파이 더 로 바이 디스 페이쓰? 낫 앳 올! 래더, 위 업호울드 더 로.
그런즉 우리가 믿음으로 말미암아 율법을 파기하느냐 그럴 수 없느니라 도리어 율법을 굳게 세우느니라

Romans 10 : 9~10

9 If you declare with your mouth, "Jesus is Lord," and believe in your heart that God raised him from the dead, you will be saved.
이프 유 디클레어 윋 요어 마우쓰, 지저스 이즈 로어드, 언드 빌리브 인 요어 하아트 댓 가드 레이즈드 힘 프럼 더 데드, 유 윌 비 세이브드.
네가 만일 네 입으로 예수를 주로 시인하며 또 하나님께서 그를 죽은 자 가운데서 살리신 것을 네 마음에 믿으면 구원을 받으리라

10 For it is with your heart that you believe and are justified, and it is with your mouth that you profess your faith and are saved.
포어 잇 이즈 윋 요어 하아트 댓 유 빌리브 언드 아아 저스터파이드, 언드 잇 이즈 윋 요어 마우쓰 댓 유 프러페스 요어 페이쓰 언드 아아 세이브드.
사람이 마음으로 믿어 의에 이르고 입으로 시인하여 구원에 이르느니라

1 Corinthians 1 : 21~24

21 For since in the wisdom of God the world through its wisdom did not know him, God was pleased through the foolishness of what was preached to save those who believe.
포어 신스 인 더 위즈덤 어브 가드 더 월드 쓰루 잇스 위즈덤 디드 낫 노우 힘, 가드 와즈 플리즈드 쓰루 더 풀리쉬너스 어브 윗 와즈 프리치트 투 세이브 도우즈 후 빌리브.
하나님의 지혜에 있어서는 이 세상이 자기 지혜로 하나님을 알지 못하므로 하나님께서 전도의 미련한 것으로 믿는 자들을 구원하시기를 기뻐하셨도다

22 Jews demand signs and Greeks look for wisdom,
주즈 디맨드 사인즈 언드 그릭스 룩 포어 위즈덤,

유대인은 표적을 구하고 헬라인은 지혜를 찾으나

23 but we preach Christ crucified: a stumbling block to Jews and foolishness to Gentiles,
벗 위 프리치 크라이스트 크루서파이드 어 스텀벌링 블락 투 주즈 언드 풀리쉬너스 투 젠타일즈,
우리는 십자가에 못 박힌 그리스도를 전하니 유대인에게는 거리끼는 것이요 이방인에게는 미련한 것이로되

24 but to those whom God has called, both Jews and Greeks, Christ the power of God and the wisdom of God.
벗 투 도우즈 훔 가드 해즈 콜드, 보우쓰 주즈 언드 그릭스, 크라이스트 더 파워 어브 가드 언드 더 위즈덤 어브 가드.
오직 부르심을 받은 자들에게는 유대인이나 헬라인이나 그리스도는 하나님의 능력이요 하나님의 지혜니라

Ephesians 2 : 8~10

8 For it is by grace you have been saved, through faith—and this is not from yourselves, it is the gift of God—
포어 잇 이즈 바이 그레이스 유 해브 빈 세이브드, 쓰루 페이쓰 언드 디스 이즈 낫 프럼 유어셀브즈, 잇 이즈 더 기프트 어브 가드
너희는 그 은혜에 의하여 믿음으로 말미암아 구원을 받았으니 이것은 너희에게서 난 것이 아니요 하나님의 선물이라

9 not by works, so that no one can boast.
낫 바이 웍스, 소우 댓 노우 원 캔 보우스트.
행위에서 난 것이 아니니 이는 누구든지 자랑하지 못하게 함이라

10 For we are God's handwork, created in Christ Jesus to do good works, which God prepared in advance for us to do.
포어 위 아아 가즈 핸드웍, 크리에이터드 인 크라이스트 지저스 투 두 구드 웍스, 위치 가드 프리페어드 인 어드밴스 포어 어스 투 두.
우리는 그가 만드신 바라 그리스도 예수 안에서 선한 일을 위하여 지으심을 받은 자니 이 일은 하나님이 전에 예비하사 우리로 그 가운데서 행하게 하려 하심이니라

Hebrews 11 : 5~6

5 By faith Enoch was taken from this life, so that he did not experience death; "He could not be found, because God had taken him away. For before he was taken, he was commended as one who pleased God.
바이 페이쓰 이넉 와즈 테이컨 프럼 디스 라이프, 소우 댓 히 디드 낫 익스피어리언스 데쓰 히 쿠드 낫 비 파운드, 비카즈 가드 해드 테이컨 힘 어웨이. 포어 비포어 히 와즈 테이컨, 히 와즈 커멘디드 애즈 원 후 플리즈드 가드.
믿음으로 에녹은 죽음을 보지 않고 옮겨졌으니 하나님이 그를 옮기심으로 다시 보이지 아니하였느니라 그는 옮겨지기 전에 하나님을 기쁘시게 하는 자라 하는 증거를 받았느니라

6 And without faith it is impossible to please God, because anyone who comes to him must believe that he exists and that he rewards those who earnestly seek him.
언드 위다우트 페이쓰 잇 이즈 임파서벌 투 플리즈 가드, 비카즈 에니원 후 컴즈 투 힘 머스트 빌리브 댓 히 이그지스트스 언드 댓 히 리워어즈 도우즈 후 어너스틀리 식 힘.
믿음이 없이는 하나님을 기쁘시게 하지 못하나니 하나님께 나아가는 자는 반드시 그가 계신 것과 또한 그가 자기를 찾는 자들에게 상 주시는 이심을 믿어야 할지니라

James 2 : 15~17

15 Suppose a brother or a sister is without clothes and daily food.
서포우즈 어 브러더 오어 어 시스터 이즈 위다우트 클로욷즈 언드 데일리 푸드.
만일 형제나 자매가 헐벗고 일용할 양식이 없는데

16 If one of you says to them, "Go, in peace; keep warm and well fed," but does nothing about their physical needs, what good is it?
이프 원 어브 유 세즈 투 뎀, 고우, 인 피스 킵 웜 언드 웰 페드, 벗 더즈 너씽 어바우트 데어 피지컬 니즈, 웟 구드 이즈 잇?
너희 중에 누구든지 그에게 이르되 평안히 가라, 덥게 하라, 배부르게 하라 하며 그 몸에 쓸 것을 주지 아니하면 무슨 유익이 있으리요

17 In the same way, faith by itself, if it is not accompanied by action, is dead.
인 더 세임 웨이, 페이쓰 바이 잇셀프, 이프 잇 이즈 낫 어컴퍼니드 바이 액션, 이즈 데드.
이와 같이 행함이 없는 믿음은 그 자체가 죽은 것이라

James 2 : 23~26

23 And the scripture was fulfilled that says, "Abraham believed God, and it was credited to him as right-
eousness," and he was called God's friend.
언드 더 스크립처 와즈 풀필드 댓 세즈, 에이브러햄 빌리브드 가드, 언드 잇 와즈 크레더터드 투 힘 애즈 라이처스너스, 언
드 히 와즈 콜드 가즈 프렌드.
이에 성경에 이른 바 아브라함이 하나님을 믿으니 이것을 의로 여기셨다는 말씀이 이루어졌고 그는 하나님의 벗이라 칭
함을 받았나니
24 You see that a person is considered righteous by what they do and not by faith alone.
유 시 댓 어 퍼선 이즈 컨시더드 라이처스 바이 왓 데이 두 언드 낫 바이 페이쓰 얼로운.
이로 보건대 사람이 행함으로 의롭다 하심을 받고 믿음으로만은 아니니라
25 In the same way, was not even Rahab the prostitute considered righteous for what she did when she
gave lodging to the spies and sent them off in a different direction?
인 더 세임 웨이, 와즈 낫 이빈 러해브 더 프라스터툿 컨시더드 라이처스 포어 왓 쉬 디드 웬 쉬 게이브 라징 투 더 스파이
즈 언드 센트 뎀 오프 인 어 디퍼런트 더렉션?
또 이와 같이 기생 라합이 사자들을 접대하여 다른 길로 나가게 할 때에 행함으로 의롭다 하심을 받은 것이 아니냐
26 As the body without the spirit is dead, so faith without deeds is dead.
애즈 더 바디 위다우트 더 스피럿 이즈 데드, 소우 페이쓰 위다우트 디즈 이즈 데드.
영혼 없는 몸이 죽은 것 같이 행함이 없는 믿음은 죽은 것이니라

1 Peter 1 : 7~9

7 These have come so that the proven genuineness of your faith—of greater worth than gold, which perishes
even though refined by fire—may result in praise, glory and honor when Jesus Christ is revealed.
디즈 해브 컴 소우 댓 더 프루번 제뉴어니스 어브 요어 페이쓰 어브 그레이터 워쓰 던 고울드, 위치 페어리쉬즈 이빈 도우
러파인드 바이 파여 메이 리절트 인 프레이즈, 글로어리 언드 아너 웬 지저스 크라이스트 이즈 리빌드.
너희 믿음의 확실함은 불로 연단하여도 없어질 금보다 더 귀하여 예수 그리스도께서 나타나실 때에 칭찬과 영광과 존귀
를 얻게 할 것이니라
8 Though you have not seen him, you love him; and even though you do not see him now, you believe in
him and are filled with an inexpressible and glorious joy,
도우 유 해브 낫 신 힘, 유 러브 힘 언드 이빈 도우 유 두 낫 시 힘 나우, 유 빌리브 인 힘 언드 아아 필드 윋 앤 이닉스프레서
벌 언드 글로어리어스 조이,
예수를 너희가 보지 못하였으나 사랑하는도다 이제도 보지 못하나 믿고 말할 수 없는 영광스러운 즐거움으로 기뻐하니
9 for you are receiving the end result of your faith, the salvation of your souls.
포어 유 아아 러시빙 디 엔드 리절트 어브 요어 페이쓰, 더 샐베이션 어브 요어 소울즈.
믿음의 결국 곧 영혼의 구원을 받음이라

1 John 5 : 10~12

10 Whoever believes in the Son of God accepts this testimony. Whoever does not believe God has made
him out to be a liar, because they have not believed the testimony God has given about his Son.
후에버 빌리브즈 인 더 선 어브 가드 액셉트스 디스 테스티모우니. 후에버 더즈 낫 빌리브 가드 해즈 메이드 힘 아웃 투 비
어 라여, 비카즈 데이 해브 낫 빌리브드 더 테스티모우니 가드 해즈 기번 어바우트 히즈 선.
하나님의 아들을 믿는 자는 자기 안에 증거가 있고 하나님을 믿지 아니하는 자는 하나님을 거짓말하는 자로 만드나니 이
는 하나님께서 그 아들에 대하여 증언하신 증거를 믿지 아니하였음이라
11 And this is the testimony: God has given us eternal life, and this life is in his Son.
언드 디스 이즈 더 테스티모우니 가드 해즈 기번 어스 이터널 라이프, 언드 디스 라이프 이즈 인 히즈 선.
또 증거는 이것이니 하나님이 우리에게 영생을 주신 것과 이 생명이 그의 아들 안에 있는 그것이니라
12 Whoever has the Son has life; whoever does not have the Son of God does not have life.
후에버 해즈 더 선 해즈 라이프 후에버 더즈 낫 해브 더 선 어브 가드 더즈 낫 해브 라이프.
아들이 있는 자에게는 생명이 있고 하나님의 아들이 없는 자에게는 생명이 없느니라

Revelation 14 : 12

12 This calls for patient endurance on the part of the people of God who keep his commands and remain faithful to Jesus.
디스 콜즈 포어 페이션트 엔더런스 안 더 파아트 어브 더 피펄 어브 가드 후 킵 히즈 커맨즈 언드 리메인 페이쓰펄 투 지저스.
성도들의 인내가 여기 있나니 그들은 하나님의 계명과 예수에 대한 믿음을 지키는 자니라

gospel [gάspəl] n. 복음	confirm [kənfə́ːrm] vt. 확증하다	boast [boust] vi. 자랑하다
Jew [dʒuː] n. 유대인	descent [disént] n. 하강	prepare [pripέər] vt. 준비하다
Gentile [dʒéntail] n. 이방인	decision [disíʒən] n. 결심	advance [ædvǽns] vt. 나아가게 하다
reveal [rivíːl] vt. 드러내다	nullify [nʌ́ləfài] vt. 파기하다	experience [ikspíəriəns] n. 경험
immediately [imíːdiətli] ad. 곧, 바로	uphold [ʌphóuld] vt. 받치다	earnestly [ə́ːrnistli] ad. 진심으로
exclaim [ikskléim] vt. 외치다	profess [prəfés] vt. 공언하다	suppose [səpóuz] vt. 가정하다
overcome [òuvərkʌ́m] vt. 극복하다	demand [dimǽnd] vt. 요구하다	endurance [indjúərəns] n. 인내

I will bless them. 내가 그들에게 복을 주리라

Numbers 6 : 24~27

24 "The LORD bless you and keep you;
더 로어드 블레스 유 언드 킵 유
여호와는 네게 복을 주시고 너를 지키시기를 원하며
25 the LORD make his face shine on you and be gracious to you;
더 로어드 메익 히즈 페이스 샤인 안 유 언드 비 그레이셔스 투 유
여호와는 그의 얼굴을 네게 비추사 은혜 베푸시기를 원하며
26 the LORD turn his face toward you and give you peace."
더 로어드 턴 히즈 페이스 터워어드 유 언드 기브 유 피스.
여호와는 그 얼굴을 네게로 향하여 드사 평강 주시기를 원하노라 할지니라 하라
27 "So they will put my name on the Israelites, and I will bless them."
소우 데이 윌 풋 마이 네임 안 디 이즈럴랏스, 언드 아이 윌 블레스 뎀.
그들은 이같이 내 이름으로 이스라엘 자손에게 축복할지니 내가 그들에게 복을 주리라

Genesis 5 : 1~2

1 This is the written account of Adam's family line. When God created mankind, he made them in the likeness of God.
디스 이즈 더 리턴 어카운트 어브 애덤즈 패멀리 라인. 웬 가드 크리에이터드 맨카인드, 히 메이드 뎀 인 더 라익너스 어브 가드.
이것은 아담의 계보를 적은 책이니라 하나님이 사람을 창조하실 때에 하나님의 모양대로 지으시되
2 He created them male and female and blessed them. And he named them "Mankind." when they were created.
히 크리에이터드 뎀 메일 언드 피메일 언드 블레스트 뎀. 언드 히 네임드 뎀 맨카인드. 웬 데이 워 크리에이터드.
남자와 여자를 창조하셨고 그들이 창조되던 날에 하나님이 그들에게 복을 주시고 그들의 이름을 사람이라 일컬으셨더라

Genesis 9 : 1~3

1 Then God blessed Noah and his sons, saying to them, "Be fruitful and increase in number and fill the earth.
덴 가드 블레스트 노우어 언드 히즈 선즈, 세이잉 투 뎀, 비 프룻펄 언드 인크리스 인 넘버 언드 필 디 어쓰.
하나님이 노아와 그 아들들에게 복을 주시며 그들에게 이르시되 생육하고 번성하여 땅에 충만하라
2 The fear and dread of you will fall on all the beasts of the earth, and on all the birds in the sky, on every creature that moves along the ground, and on all the fish in the sea; they are given into your hands.

더 피어 언드 드레드 어브 유 윌 폴 안 올 더 비스트스 어브 디 어쓰, 언드 안 올 더 버즈 인 더 스카이, 안 에브리 크리처 댓 무브즈 얼롱 더 그라운드, 언드 안 올 더 피쉬 인 더 시 데이 아아 기번 인투 요어 핸즈.
땅의 모든 짐승과 공중의 모든 새와 땅에 기는 모든 것과 바다의 모든 물고기가 너희를 두려워하며 너희를 무서워하리니 이것들은 너희의 손에 붙였음이니라

3 Everything that lives and moves about will be food for you. Just as I gave you the green plants, I now give you everything.
에브리씽 댓 라이브즈 언드 무브즈 어바우트 윌 비 푸드 포어 유. 저스트 애즈 아이 게이브 유 더 그린 플랜트스, 아이 나우 기브 유 에브리씽.
모든 산 동물은 너희의 먹을 것이 될지라 채소 같이 내가 이것을 다 너희에게 주노라

Genesis 22 : 16~18

16 and said, "I swear by myself, declares the LORD, that because you have done this and have not withheld your son, your only son,
언드 세드, 아이 스웨어 바이 마이셀프, 디클레어즈 더 로어드, 댓 비카즈 유 해브 던 디스 언드 해브 낫 위쓰헬드 요어 선, 요어 오운리 선,
이르시되 여호와께서 이르시기를 내가 나를 가리켜 맹세하노니 네가 이같이 행하여 네 아들 네 독자도 아끼지 아니하였은즉

17 I will surely bless you and make your descendants as numerous as the stars in the sky and as the sand on the seashore. Your descendants will take possession of the cities of their enemies,
아이 윌 슈얼리 블레스 유 언드 메익 요어 디센던트스 애즈 누머러스 애즈 더 스타아즈 인 더 스카이 언드 애즈 더 샌드 안 더 시쇼어. 요어 디센던트스 윌 테익 퍼제션 어브 더 시티즈 어브 데어 에너미즈,
내가 네게 큰 복을 주고 네 씨가 크게 번성하여 하늘의 별과 같고 바닷가의 모래와 같게 하리니 네 씨가 그 대적의 성문을 차지하리라

18 and through your offspring all nations on earth will be blessed, because you have obeyed me."
언드 쓰루 요어 오프스프링 올 네이션즈 안 어쓰 윌 비 블레스트, 비카즈 유 해브 오우베이드 미.
또 네 씨로 말미암아 천하 만민이 복을 받으리니 이는 네가 나의 말을 준행하였음이니라 하셨다 하니라

Deuteronomy 28 : 1~6

1 If you fully obey the LORD your God and carefully follow all his commands I give you today, the LORD your God will set you high above all the nations on earth.
이프 유 풀리 오우베이 더 로어드 요어 가드 언드 케어펄리 팔로우 올 히즈 커맨즈 아이 기브 유 터데이, 더 로어드 요어 가드 윌 셋 유 하이 어버브 올 더 네이션즈 안 어쓰.
네가 네 하나님 여호와의 말씀을 삼가 듣고 내가 오늘 네게 명령하는 그의 모든 명령을 지켜 행하면 네 하나님 여호와께서 너를 세계 모든 민족 위에 뛰어나게 하실 것이라

2 All these blessings will come on you and accompany you if you obey the LORD your God:
올 디즈 블레싱즈 윌 컴 안 유 언드 어컴퍼니 유 이프 유 오우베이 더 로어드 요어 가드
네가 네 하나님 여호와의 말씀을 청종하면 이 모든 복이 네게 임하며 네게 이르리니

3 You will be blessed in the city and blessed in the country.
유 윌 비 블레스트 인 더 시티 언드 블레스트 인 더 컨트리.
성읍에서도 복을 받고 들에서도 복을 받을 것이며

4 The fruit of your womb will be blessed, and the crops of your land and the young of your livestock—the calves of your herds and the lambs of your flocks.
더 프룻 어브 요어 웜 윌 비 블레스트, 언드 더 크랍스 어브 요어 랜드 언드 더 영 어브 요어 라이브스탁 더 캐브즈 어브 요어 허즈 언드 더 램즈 어브 요어 플락스.
네 몸의 자녀와 네 토지의 소산과 네 짐승의 새끼와 소와 양의 새끼가 복을 받을 것이며

5 Your basket and your kneading trough will be blessed.
요어 배스컷 언드 요어 니딩 트로프 윌 비 블레스트.
네 광주리와 떡 반죽 그릇이 복을 받을 것이며

6 You will be blessed when you come in and blessed when you go out.

유 윌 비 블레스트 웬 유 컴 인 언드 블레스트 웬 유 고우 아웃.
네가 들어와도 복을 받고 나가도 복을 받을 것이니라

Psalms 1 : 1~6

1 Blessed is the one who does not walk in step with the wicked or stand in the way that sinners take or sit in the company of mockers,
블레스트 이즈 더 원 후 더즈 낫 웍 인 스텝 윋 더 위커드 오어 스탠드 인 더 웨이 댓 시너즈 테익 오어 싯 인 더 컴퍼니 어브 마커즈,
복 있는 사람은 악인들의 꾀를 따르지 아니하며 죄인들의 길에 서지 아니하며 오만한 자들의 자리에 앉지 아니하고

2 but whose delight is in the law of the LORD, and who meditates on his law day and night.
벗 후즈 딜랏 이즈 인 더 로 어브 더 로어드, 언드 후 메더테잇스 안 히즈 로 데이 언드 나이트.
오직 여호와의 율법을 즐거워하여 그의 율법을 주야로 묵상하는도다

3 That person is like a tree planted by streams of water, which yields its fruit in season and whose leaf does not wither—whatever they do prospers.
댓 퍼선 이즈 라익 어 트리 플랜터드 바이 스트림즈 어브 워터, 위치 일즈 잇스 프룻 인 시전 언드 후즈 리프 더즈 낫 위더 워테버 데이 두 프라스퍼즈.
그는 시냇가에 심은 나무가 철을 따라 열매를 맺으며 그 잎사귀가 마르지 아니함 같으니 그가 하는 모든 일이 다 형통하리로다

4 Not so the wicked! They are like chaff that the wind blows away.
낫 소우 더 위커드! 데이 아아 라익 채프 댓 더 윈드 블로우즈 어웨이.
악인들은 그렇지 아니함이여 오직 바람에 나는 겨와 같도다

5 Therefore the wicked will not stand in the judgment, nor sinners in the assembly of the righteous.
데어포어 더 위커드 윌 낫 스탠드 인 더 저지먼트, 노어 시너즈 인 디 어셈블리 어브 더 라이처스.
그러므로 악인들은 심판을 견디지 못하며 죄인들이 의인들의 모임에 들지 못하리로다

6 For the LORD watches over the way of the righteous, but the way of the wicked leads to destruction.
포어 더 로어드 와처즈 오우버 더 웨이 어브 더 라이처스, 벗 더 웨이 어브 더 위커드 리즈 투 디스트럭션.
무릇 의인들의 길은 여호와께서 인정하시나 악인들의 길은 망하리로다

Proverbs 3 : 13~20

13 Blessed are those who find wisdom, those who gain understanding,
블레스트 아아 도우즈 후 파인드 위즈덤, 도우즈 후 게인 언더스탠딩,
지혜를 얻은 자와 명철을 얻은 자는 복이 있나니

14 for she is more profitable than silver and yields better returns than gold.
포어 쉬 이즈 모어 프라퍼터벌 던 실버 언드 일즈 베터 리턴즈 던 고울드.
이는 지혜를 얻는 것이 은을 얻는 것보다 낫고 그 이익이 정금보다 나음이니라

15 She is more precious than rubies; nothing you desire can compare with her.
쉬 이즈 모어 프레셔스 던 루비즈 너씽 유 디자여 캔 컴페어 윋 허.
지혜는 진주보다 귀하니 네가 사모하는 모든 것으로도 이에 비교할 수 없도다

16 Long life is in her right hand; in her left hand are riches and honor.
롱 라이프 이즈 인 허 라이트 핸드 인 허 레프트 핸드 아아 리처즈 언드 아너.
그의 오른손에는 장수가 있고 그의 왼손에는 부귀가 있나니

17 Her ways are pleasant ways, and all her paths are peace.
허 웨이즈 아아 플레전트 웨이즈, 언드 올 허 팬즈 아아 피스.
그 길은 즐거운 길이요 그의 지름길은 다 평강이니라

18 She is a tree of life to those who take hold of her; those who hold her fast will be blessed.
쉬 이즈 어 트리 어브 라이프 투 도우즈 후 테익 호울드 어브 허 도우즈 후 호울드 허 패스트 윌 비 블레스트.
지혜는 그 얻은 자에게 생명 나무라 지혜를 가진 자는 복되도다

19 By wisdom the LORD laid the earth's foundations, by understanding he set the heavens in place;

바이 위즈덤 더 로어드 레이드 디 어쓰스 파운데이션즈, 바이 언더스탠딩 히 셋 더 헤번즈 인 플레이스
여호와께서는 지혜로 땅에 터를 놓으셨으며 명철로 하늘을 견고히 세우셨고

20 by his knowledge the watery depths were divided, and the clouds let drop the dew.
바이 히즈 날러지 더 워터리 뎁쓰스 워 디바이디드, 언드 더 클라우즈 렛 드랍 더 두.
그의 지식으로 깊은 바다를 갈라지게 하셨으며 공중에서 이슬이 내리게 하셨느니라

Malachi 3 : 10~12

10 Bring the whole tithe into the storehouse, that there may be food in my house. Test me in this," says the LORD Almighty, " and see if I will not throw open the floodgates of heaven and pour out so much blessing that there will not be room enough to store it.
브링 더 호울 타읻 인투 더 스토어하우스, 댓 데어 메이 비 푸드 인 마이 하우스. 테스트 미 인 디스, 세즈 더 로어드 올마이티, 언드 시 이프 아이 윌 낫 쓰로우 오우펀 더 플러드게잇스 어브 헤번 언드 포어 아웃 소우 머치 블레싱 댓 데어 윌 낫 비 룸 이너프 투 스토어 잇.
만군의 여호와가 이르노라 너희의 온전한 십일조를 창고에 들여 나의 집에 양식이 있게 하고 그것으로 나를 시험하여 내가 하늘 문을 열고 너희에게 복을 쌓을 곳이 없도록 붓지 아니하나 보라

11 I will prevent pests from devouring your crops, and the vines in your fields will not drop their fruit before it is ripe," says the LORD Almighty.
아이 윌 프리벤트 페스트스 프럼 디바워잉 요어 크랍스, 언드 더 바인즈 인 요어 필즈 윌 낫 드랍 데어 프룻 비포어 잇 이즈 라입, 세즈 더 로어드 올마이티.
만군의 여호와가 이르노라 내가 너희를 위하여 메뚜기를 금하여 너희 토지 소산을 먹어 없애지 못하게 하며 너희 밭의 포도나무 열매가 기한 전에 떨어지지 않게 하리니

12 "Then all the nations will call you blessed, for yours will be a delightful land," says the LORD Almighty.
덴 올 더 네이션즈 윌 콜 유 블레스트, 포어 유어즈 윌 비 어 딜랏펄 랜드, 세즈 더 로어드 올마이티.
너희 땅이 아름다워지므로 모든 이방인들이 너희를 복되다 하리라 만군의 여호와의 말이니라

Matthew 5 : 3~12

3 "Blessed are the poor in spirit, for theirs is the kingdom of heaven.
블레스트 아아 더 푸어 인 스피릿, 포어 데어즈 이즈 더 킹덤 어브 헤번.
심령이 가난한 자는 복이 있나니 천국이 그들의 것임이요

4 Blessed are those who mourn, for they will be comforted.
블레스트 아아 도우즈 후 몬, 포어 데이 윌 비 컴퍼티드.
애통하는 자는 복이 있나니 그들이 위로를 받을 것임이요

5 Blessed are the meek, for they will inherit the earth.
블레스트 아아 더 믹, 포어 데이 윌 인헤럿 디 어쓰.
온유한 자는 복이 있나니 그들이 땅을 기업으로 받을 것임이요

6 Blessed are those who hunger and thirst for righteousness, for they will be filled.
블레스트 아아 도우즈 후 헝거 언드 써스트 포어 라이처스너스, 포어 데이 윌 비 필드.
의에 주리고 목마른 자는 복이 있나니 그들이 배부를 것임이요

7 Blessed are the merciful, for they will be shown mercy.
블레스트 아아 더 머시펄, 포어 데이 윌 비 쇼운 머시.
긍휼히 여기는 자는 복이 있나니 그들이 긍휼히 여김을 받을 것임이요

8 Blessed are the pure in heart, for they will see God.
블레스트 아아 더 풀 인 하아트, 포어 데이 윌 시 가드.
마음이 청결한 자는 복이 있나니 그들이 하나님을 볼 것임이요

9 Blessed are the peacemakers, for they will be called children of God.
블레스트 아아 더 피스메이커즈, 포어 데이 윌 비 콜드 칠드런 어브 가드.
화평하게 하는 자는 복이 있나니 그들이 하나님의 아들이라 일컬음을 받을 것임이요

10 Blessed are those who are persecuted because of righteousness, for theirs is the kingdom of heaven.

블레스트 아아 도우즈 후 아아 퍼서큐터드 비카즈 어브 라이처스너스, 포어 데어즈 이즈 더 킹덤 어브 헤번.
의를 위하여 박해를 받은 자는 복이 있나니 천국이 그들의 것임이라
11 "Blessed are you when people insult you, persecute you and falsely say all kinds of evil against you be-
cause of me.
블레스트 아아 유 웬 피펄 인설트 유, 퍼서큣 유 언드 폴슬리 세이 올 카인즈 어브 이벌 어겐스트 유 비카즈 어브 미.
나로 말미암아 너희를 욕하고 박해하고 거짓으로 너희를 거슬러 모든 악한 말을 할 때에는 너희에게 복이 있나니
12 Rejoice and be glad, because great is your reward in heaven, for in the same way they persecuted the
prophets who were before you.
리조이스 언드 비 글래드, 비카즈 그레이트 이즈 요어 리워어드 인 헤번, 포어 인 더 세임 웨이 데이 퍼서큐터드 더 프라펏
스 후 워 비포어 유.
기뻐하고 즐거워하라 하늘에서 너희의 상이 큼이라 너희 전에 있던 선지자들도 이같이 박해하였느니라

bless [bles] vt. …에게 은총을 내리다	seashore [síːʃɔ̀ːr] n. 해변	assembly [əsémbli] n. 집회
shine [ʃain] vt. 비추다	offspring [ɔ́(ː)fsprìŋ] n. 자식	destruction [distrʌ́kʃən] n. 파괴
likeness [láiknis] n. 닮음	obey [oubéi] vi. 복종하다	profitable [prɑ́fitəbəl] a. 유리한
increase [inkríːs] vt. 늘리다	livestock [láiv-] n. 가축류	foundation [faundéiʃən] n. 창설
beast [biːst] n. 짐승	knead [niːd] vt. 반죽하다	depth [depθ] n. 깊이
withhold [wiðhóuld] vt. 보류하다	meditate [médətèit] vi. 명상하다	storehouse [stɔːrhaus] n. 창고
descendant [diséndənt] n. 자손	prosper [prɑ́spər] vi. 번영하다	persecute [pə́ːrsikjùːt] vt. 박해하다

You may be careful to do everything written in it. 그 안에 기록된 대로 다 지켜 행하라

Joshua 1 : 8~9

8 Keep this Book of the Law always on your lips; meditate on it day and night, so that you may be careful
to do everything written in it. Then you will be prosperous and successful.
킵 디스 북 어브 더 로 올웨이즈 안 요어 립스 메더테이트 안 잇 데이 언드 나이트, 소우 댓 유 메이 비 케어펄 투 두 에브리
씽 리턴 인 잇. 덴 유 윌 비 프라스퍼러스 언드 석세스펄.
이 율법책을 네 입에서 떠나지 말게 하며 주야로 그것을 묵상하여 그 안에 기록된 대로 다 지켜 행하라 그리하면 네 길이
평탄하게 될 것이며 네가 형통하리라
9 Have I not commanded you? Be strong and courageous. Do not be afraid; do not be discouraged, for the
LORD your God will be with you wherever you go."
해브 아이 낫 커맨디드 유? 비 스트롱 언드 커리저스. 두 낫 비 어프레이드 두 낫 비 디스커리지드, 포어 더 로어드 요어 가
드 윌 비 윋 유 웨레버 유 고우.
내가 네게 명령한 것이 아니냐 강하고 담대하라 두려워하지 말며 놀라지 말라 네가 어디로 가든지 네 하나님 여호와가 너
와 함께 하느니라 하시니라

Exodus 12 : 13~14

13 The blood will be a sign for you on the houses where you are; and when I see the blood, I will pass over
you. No destructive plague will touch you when I strike Egypt.
더 블러드 윌 비 어 사인 포어 유 안 더 하우서즈 웨어 유 아아 언드 웬 아이 시 더 블러드, 아이 윌 패스 오우버 유. 노우 디
스트럭티브 플레이그 윌 터치 유 웬 아이 스트라익 이접트.
내가 애굽 땅을 칠 때에 그 피가 너희가 사는 집에 있어서 너희를 위하여 표적이 될지라 내가 피를 볼 때에 너희를 넘어
가리니 재앙이 너희에게 내려 멸하지 아니하리라
14 "This is a day you are to commemorate; for the generations to come you shall celebrate it as a festival to
the LORD—a lasting ordinance.
디스 이즈 어 데이 유 아아 투 커메머레잍 포어 더 제너레이션즈 투 컴 유 섈 셀러브레이트 잇 애즈 어 페스터벌 투 더 로
어드 에이 래스팅 오어더넌스.
너희는 이 날을 기념하여 여호와의 절기를 삼아 영원한 규례로 대대로 지킬지니라

Exodus 15 : 26

26 He said, "If you listen carefully to the LORD your God and do what is right in his eyes, if you pay attention to his commands and keep all his decrees, I will not bring on you any of the diseases I brought on the Egyptians, for I am the LORD, who heals you."
히 세드, 이프 유 리선 케어펄리 투 더 로어드 요어 가드 언드 두 웟 이즈 라이트 인 히즈 아이즈, 이프 유 페이 어텐션 투 히즈 커맨즈 언드 킵 올 히즈 디크리즈, 아이 윌 낫 브링 안 유 에니 어브 더 디지저즈 아이 브롯 안 디 이집션즈, 포어 아이 앰 더 로어드, 후 힐즈 유.
이르시되 너희가 너희 하나님 나 여호와의 말을 들어 순종하고 내가 보기에 의를 행하며 내 계명에 귀를 기울이며 내 모든 규례를 지키면 내가 애굽 사람에게 내린 모든 질병 중 하나도 너희에게 내리지 아니하리니 나는 너희를 치료하는 여호와임이라

Exodus 19 : 5~6

5 Now if you obey me fully and keep my covenant, then out of all nations you will be my treasured possession. Although the whole earth is mine,
나우 이프 유 오우베이 미 풀리 언드 킵 마이 커버넌트, 덴 아웃 어브 올 네이션즈 유 윌 비 마이 트레저드 퍼제션. 올도우 더 호울 어쓰 이즈 마인,
세계가 다 내게 속하였나니 너희가 내 말을 잘 듣고 내 언약을 지키면 너희는 모든 민족 중에서 내 소유가 되겠고

6 you will be for me a kingdom of priests and a holy nation.' These are the words you are to speak to the Israelites."
유 윌 비 포어 미 어 킹덤 어브 프리스트스 언드 어 호울리 네이션. 디즈 아아 더 워즈 유 아아 투 스픽 투 디 이즈럴랏스.
너희가 내게 대하여 제사장 나라가 되며 거룩한 백성이 되리라 너는 이 말을 이스라엘 자손에게 전할지니라

Exodus 20 : 1~17

1 And God spoke all these words:
언드 가드 스포욱 올 디즈 워즈
하나님이 이 모든 말씀으로 말씀하여 이르시되

2 "I am the LORD your God, who brought you out of Egypt, out of the land of slavery.
아이 앰 더 로어드 요어 가드, 후 브롯 유 아웃 어브 이접트, 아웃 어브 더 랜드 어브 슬레이버리.
나는 너를 애굽 땅, 종 되었던 집에서 인도하여 낸 네 하나님 여호와니라

3 "You shall have no other gods before me.
유 섈 해브 노우 어더 가즈 비포 미.
너는 나 외에는 다른 신들을 네게 두지 말라

4 "You shall not make for yourself an image in the form of anything in heaven above or on the earth beneath or in the waters below.
유 섈 낫 메익 포어 요어셀프 앤 이머지 인 더 폼 어브 에니씽 인 헤번 어버브 오어 안 디 어쓰 비니쓰 오어 인 더 워터즈 빌로우.
너를 위하여 새긴 우상을 만들지 말고 또 위로 하늘에 있는 것이나 아래로 땅에 있는 것이나 땅 아래 물 속에 있는 것의 어떤 형상도 만들지 말며

5 You shall not bow down to them or worship them; for I, the LORD your God, am a jealous God, punishing the children for the sin of the parents to the third and fourth generation of those who hate me,
유 섈 낫 바우 다운 투 뎀 오어 워셥 뎀 포어 아이, 더 로어드 요어 가드, 앰 어 젤러스 가드, 퍼니쉉 더 칠드런 포어 더 신 어브 더 페런트스 투 더 써드 언드 포어쓰 제너레이션 어브 도우즈 후 헤이트 미,
그것들에게 절하지 말며 그것들을 섬기지 말라 나 네 하나님 여호와는 질투하는 하나님인즉 나를 미워하는 자의 죄를 갚되 아버지로부터 아들에게로 삼사 대까지 이르게 하거니와

6 but showing love to a thousand generations of those who love me and keep my commandments.
벗 쇼우잉 러브 투 어 싸우전드 제너레이션즈 어브 도우즈 후 러브 미 언드 킵 마이 커맨드먼트스.
나를 사랑하고 내 계명을 지키는 자에게는 천 대까지 은혜를 베푸느니라

7 "You shall not misuse the name of the LORD your God, for the LORD will not hold anyone guiltless who misuses his name.
유 섈 낫 미스유즈 더 네임 어브 더 로어드 요어 가드, 포어 더 로어드 윌 낫 호울드 에니원 길틀리스 후 미스유지즈 히즈 네임.
너는 네 하나님 여호와의 이름을 망령되게 부르지 말라 여호와는 그의 이름을 망령되게 부르는 자를 죄 없다 하지 아니하리라
8 "Remember the Sabbath day by keeping it holy.
리멤버 더 새버쓰 데이 바이 키핑 잇 호울리.
안식일을 기억하여 거룩하게 지키라
9 Six days you shall labor and do all your work,
식스 데이즈 유 섈 레이버 언드 두 올 요어 웍,
엿새 동안은 힘써 네 모든 일을 행할 것이나
10 but the seventh day is a sabbath to the LORD your God. On it you shall not do any work, neither you, nor your son or daughter, nor your male or female servant, nor your animals, nor any foreigner residing in your towns.
벗 더 세번쓰 데이 이즈 어 새버쓰 투 더 로어드 요어 가드. 안 잇 유 섈 낫 두 에니 웍, 나이더 유, 노어 요어 선 오어 도터, 노어 요어 메일 오어 피메일 서번트, 노어 요어 애너멀즈, 노어 에니 포러너 리자이딩 인 요어 타운즈.
일곱째 날은 네 하나님 여호와의 안식일인즉 너나 네 아들이나 네 딸이나 네 남종이나 네 여종이나 네 가축이나 네 문안에 머무는 객이라도 아무 일도 하지 말라
11 For in six days the LORD made the heavens and the earth, the sea, and all that is in them, but he rested on the seventh day. Therefore the LORD blessed the Sabbath day and made it holy.
포어 인 식스 데이즈 더 로어드 메이드 더 헤번즈 언드 디 어쓰, 더 시, 언드 올 댓 이즈 인 뎀, 벗 히 레스터드 안 더 세번쓰 데이. 데어포어 더 로어드 블레스트 더 새버쓰 데이 언드 메이드 잇 호울리.
이는 엿새 동안에 나 여호와가 하늘과 땅과 바다와 그 가운데 모든 것을 만들고 일곱째 날에 쉬었음이라 그러므로 나 여호와가 안식일을 복되게 하여 그 날을 거룩하게 하였느니라
12 "Honor your father and your mother, so that you may live long in the land the LORD your God is giving you.
아너 요어 파더 언드 요어 머더, 소우 댓 유 메이 리브 롱 인 더 랜드 더 로어드 요어 가드 이즈 기빙 유.
네 부모를 공경하라 그리하면 네 하나님 여호와가 네게 준 땅에서 네 생명이 길리라
13 "You shall not murder.
유 섈 낫 머더.
살인하지 말라
14 "You shall not commit adultery.
유 섈 낫 커밋 어덜터리.
간음하지 말라
15 "You shall not steal.
유 섈 낫 스틸.
도둑질하지 말라
16 "You shall not give false testimony against your neighbor.
유 섈 낫 기브 폴스 테스티모우니 어겐스트 요어 네이버.
네 이웃에 대하여 거짓 증거하지 말라
17 "You shall not covet your neighbor's house. You shall not covet your neighbor's wife, or his male or female servant, his ox or donkey, or anything that belongs to your neighbor."
유 섈 낫 커벗 요어 네이버즈 하우스. 유 섈 낫 커벗 요어 네이버즈 와이프, 오어 히즈 메일 오어 피메일 서번트 , 히즈 악스 오어 당키, 오어 에니씽 댓 빌롱즈 투 요어 네이버.
네 이웃의 집을 탐내지 말라 네 이웃의 아내나 그의 남종이나 그의 여종이나 그의 소나 그의 나귀나 무릇 네 이웃의 소유를 탐내지 말라

Deuteronomy 6 : 1~3

1 These are the commands, decrees and laws the LORD your God directed me to teach you to observe in

the land that you are crossing the Jordan to possess,
디즈 아아 더 커맨즈, 디크리즈 언드 로즈 더 로어드 요어 가드 더렉터드 미 투 티치 유 투 어브저브 인 더 랜드 댓 유 아아 크로싱 더 조어던 투 퍼제스,
이는 곧 너희의 하나님 여호와께서 너희에게 가르치라고 명하신 명령과 규례와 법도라 너희가 건너가서 차지할 땅에서 행할 것이니

2 so that you, your children and their children after them may fear the LORD your God as long as you live by keeping all his decrees and commands that I give you, and so that you may enjoy long life.
소우 댓 유, 요어 칠드런 언드 데어 칠드런 애프터 뎀 메이 피어 더 로어드 요어 가드 애즈 롱 애즈 유 라이브 바이 키핑 올 히즈 디크리즈 언드 커맨즈 댓 아이 기브 유, 언드 소우 댓 유 메이 엔조이 롱 라이프.
곧 너와 네 아들과 네 손자들이 평생에 네 하나님 여호와를 경외하며 내가 너희에게 명한 그 모든 규례와 명령을 지키게 하기 위한 것이며 또 네 날을 장구하게 하기 위한 것이라

3 Hear, Israel, and be careful to obey so that it may go well with you and that you may increase greatly in a land flowing with milk and honey, just as the LORD, the God of your ancestors, promised you.
히어, 이즈리얼, 언드 비 케어펄 투 오우베이 소우 댓 잇 메이 고우 웰 윋 유 언드 댓 유 메이 인크리스 그레잇리 인 어 랜드 플로우잉 윋 밀크 언드 허니, 저스트 애즈 더 로어드, 더 가드 어브 요어 앤세스터즈, 프라머스트 유.
이스라엘아 듣고 삼가 그것을 행하라 그리하면 네가 복을 받고 네 조상들의 하나님 여호와께서 네게 허락하심 같이 젖과 꿀이 흐르는 땅에서 네가 크게 번성하리라

Proverbs 3 : 1~10

1 My son, do not forget my teaching, but keep my commands in your heart,
마이 선, 두 낫 퍼겟 마이 티칭, 벗 킵 마이 커맨즈 인 요어 하아트,
내 아들아 나의 법을 잊어버리지 말고 네 마음으로 나의 명령을 지키라

2 for they will prolong your life many years and bring you peace and prosperity.
포어 데이 윌 프럴롱 요어 라이프 메니 이어즈 언드 브링 유 피스 언드 프라스페러티.
그리하면 그것이 네가 장수하여 많은 해를 누리게 하며 평강을 더하게 하리라

3 Let love and faithfulness never leave you; bind them around your neck, write them on the tablet of your heart.
렛 러브 언드 페이쓰펄네스 네버 리브 유 바인드 뎀 어라운드 요어 넥, 라이트 뎀 안 더 태블럿 어브 요어 하아트.
인자와 진리가 네게서 떠나지 말게 하고 그것을 네 목에 매며 네 마음판에 새기라

4 Then you will win favor and a good name in the sight of God and man.
덴 유 윌 윈 페이버 언드 어 구드 네임 인 더 사이트 어브 가드 언드 맨.
그리하면 네가 하나님과 사람 앞에서 은총과 귀중히 여김을 받으리라

5 Trust in the LORD with all your heart and lean not on your own understanding;
트러스트 인 더 로어드 윋 올 요어 하아트 언드 린 낫 안 요어 오운 언더스탠딩
너는 마음을 다하여 여호와를 신뢰하고 네 명철을 의지하지 말라

6 in all your ways submit to him, and he will make your paths straight.
인 올 요어 웨이즈 서브밋 투 힘, 언드 히 윌 메익 요어 팬즈 스트레이트.
너는 범사에 그를 인정하라 그리하면 네 길을 지도하시리라

7 Do not be wise in your own eyes; fear the LORD and shun evil.
두 낫 비 와이즈 인 요어 오운 아이즈 피어 더 로어드 언드 션 이벌.
스스로 지혜롭게 여기지 말지어다 여호와를 경외하며 악을 떠날지어다

8 This will bring health to your body and nourishment to your bones.
디스 윌 브링 헬쓰 투 요어 바디 언드 너리쉬먼트 투 요어 보운즈.
이것이 네 몸에 양약이 되어 네 골수를 윤택하게 하리라

9 Honor the LORD with your wealth, with the firstfruits of all your crops;
아너 더 로어드 윋 요어 웰쓰, 윋 더 퍼스트프룻스 어브 올 요어 크랍스
네 재물과 네 소산물의 처음 익은 열매로 여호와를 공경하라

10 then your barns will be filled to overflowing, and your vats will brim over with new wine.
덴 요어 반즈 윌 비 필드 투 오우버플로우잉, 언드 요어 뱃스 윌 브림 오우버 윋 누 와인.
그리하면 네 창고가 가득히 차고 네 포도즙 틀에 새 포도즙이 넘치리라

Matthew 5 : 17~20

17 "Do not think that I have come to abolish the Law or the Prophets; I have not come to abolish them but to fulfill them.
두 낫 씽크 댓 아이 해브 컴 투 어발리쉬 더 로 오어 더 프라펏스 아이 해브 낫 컴 투 어발리쉬 뎀 벗 투 풀필 뎀.
내가 율법이나 선지자를 폐하러 온 줄로 생각하지 말라 폐하러 온 것이 아니요 완전하게 하려 함이라

18 For truly I tell you, until heaven and earth disappear, not the smallest letter, not the least stroke of a pen, will by any means disappear from the Law until everything is accomplished.
포어 트룰리 아이 텔 유, 언틸 헤번 언드 어쓰 디서피어, 낫 더 스몰러스트 레터, 낫 더 리스트 스트로욱 어브 어 펜, 윌 바이 에니 민즈 디서피어 프럼 더 로 언틸 에브리씽 이즈 어캄플리쉬트.
진실로 너희에게 이르노니 천지가 없어지기 전에는 율법의 일점 일획도 결코 없어지지 아니하고 다 이루리라

19 Therefore anyone who sets aside one of the least of these commands and teaches others accordingly will be called least in the kingdom of heaven, but whoever practices and teaches these commands will be called great in the kingdom of heaven.
데어포어 에니원 후 셋스 어사이드 원 어브 더 리스트 어브 디즈 커맨즈 언드 티처즈 어더즈 어코어딩리 윌 비 콜드 리스트 인 더 킹덤 어브 헤번, 벗 후에버 프랙티시즈 언드 티처즈 디즈 커맨즈 윌 비 콜드 그레이트 인 더 킹덤 어브 헤번.
그러므로 누구든지 이 계명 중의 지극히 작은 것 하나라도 버리고 또 그같이 사람을 가르치는 자는 천국에서 지극히 작다 일컬음을 받을 것이요 누구든지 이를 행하며 가르치는 자는 천국에서 크다 일컬음을 받으리라

20 For I tell you that unless your righteousness surpasses that of the Pharisees and the teachers of the law, you will certainly not enter the kingdom of heaven.
포어 아이 텔 유 댓 언레스 요어 라이처스너스 서패시즈 댓 어브 더 패어리시즈 언드 더 티처즈 어브 더 로, 유 윌 서터늘리 낫 엔터 더 킹덤 어브 헤번.
내가 너희에게 이르노니 너희 의가 서기관과 바리새인보다 더 낫지 못하면 결코 천국에 들어가지 못하리라

Matthew 7 : 24~27

24 "Therefore everyone who hears these words of mine and puts them into practice is like a wise man who built his house on the rock.
데어포어 에브리원 후 히어즈 디즈 워즈 어브 마인 언드 풋스 뎀 인투 프랙티스 이즈 라익 어 와이즈 맨 후 빌트 히즈 하우스 안 더 락.
그러므로 누구든지 나의 이 말을 듣고 행하는 자는 그 집을 반석 위에 지은 지혜로운 사람 같으리니

25 The rain came down, the streams rose, and the winds blew and beat against that house; yet it did not fall, because it had its foundation on the rock.
더 레인 케임 다운, 더 스트림즈 로우즈, 언드 더 윈즈 블루 언드 빗 어겐스트 댓 하우스 옛 잇 디드 낫 폴, 비카즈 잇 해드 잇스 파운데이션 안 더 락.
비가 내리고 창수가 나고 바람이 불어 그 집에 부딪치되 무너지지 아니하나니 이는 주추를 반석 위에 놓은 까닭이요

26 But everyone who hears these words of mine and does not put them into practice is like a foolish man who built his house on sand.
벗 에브리원 후 히어즈 디즈 워즈 어브 마인 언드 더즈 낫 풋 뎀 인투 프랙티스 이즈 라익 어 풀리쉬 맨 후 빌트 히즈 하우스 안 샌드.
나의 이 말을 듣고 행하지 아니하는 자는 그 집을 모래 위에 지은 어리석은 사람 같으리니

27 The rain came down, the streams rose, and the winds blew and beat against that house, and it fell with a great crash."
더 레인 케임 다운, 더 스트림즈 로우즈, 언드 더 윈즈 블루 언드 빗 어겐스트 댓 하우스, 언드 잇 펠 윋 어 그레이트 크래쉬.
비가 내리고 창수가 나고 바람이 불어 그 집에 부딪치매 무너져 그 무너짐이 심하니라

Matthew 28 : 18~20

18 Then Jesus came to them and said, "All authority in heaven and on earth has been given to me.
덴 지저스 케임 투 뎀 언드 세드, 올 어쏘러티 인 헤번 언드 안 어쓰 해즈 빈 기번 투 미.
예수께서 나아와 말씀하여 이르시되 하늘과 땅의 모든 권세를 내게 주셨으니

19 Therefore go and make disciples of all nations, baptizing them in the name of the Father and of the Son and of the Holy Spirit,
데어포어 고우 언드 메익 디사이펄즈 어브 올 네이션즈, 뱁타이징 뎀 인 더 네임 어브 더 파더 언드 어브 더 선 언드 어브 더 호울리 스피럿,
그러므로 너희는 가서 모든 민족을 제자로 삼아 아버지와 아들과 성령의 이름으로 세례를 베풀고

20 and teaching them to obey everything I have commanded you. And surely I am with you always, to the very end of the age."
언드 티칭 뎀 투 오우베이 에브리씽 아이 해브 커맨디드 유. 언드 슈얼리 아이 앰 윋 유 올웨이즈, 투 더 베어리 엔드 어브 디 에이지.
내가 너희에게 분부한 모든 것을 가르쳐 지키게 하라 볼지어다 내가 세상 끝날까지 너희와 항상 함께 있으리라 하시니라

Mark 4 : 14~20

14 The farmer sows the word.
더 파아머 소우즈 더 워드.
뿌리는 자는 말씀을 뿌리는 것이라

15 Some people are like seed along the path, where the word is sown. As soon as they hear it, Satan comes and takes away the word that was sown in them.
섬 피펄 아아 라익 시드 얼롱 더 패쓰, 웨어 더 워드 이즈 소운. 애즈 순 애즈 데이 히어 잇, 세이턴 컴즈 언드 테익스 어웨이 더 워드 댓 와즈 소운 인 뎀.
말씀이 길 가에 뿌려졌다는 것은 이들을 가리킴이니 곧 말씀을 들었을 때에 사탄이 즉시 와서 그들에게 뿌려진 말씀을 빼앗는 것이요

16 Others, like seed sown on rocky places, hear the word and at once receive it with joy.
어더즈, 라익 시드 소운 안 라키 플레이서즈, 히어 더 워드 언드 앳 원스 러시브 잇 윋 조이.
또 이와 같이 돌밭에 뿌려졌다는 것은 이들을 가리킴이니 곧 말씀을 들을 때에 즉시 기쁨으로 받으나

17 But since they have no root, they last only a short time. When trouble or persecution comes because of the word, they quickly fall away.
벗 신스 데이 해브 노우 룻, 데이 래스트 오운리 어 쇼어트 타임. 웬 트러벌 오어 퍼서큐션 컴즈 비카즈 어브 더 워드, 데이 퀵리 폴 어웨이.
그 속에 뿌리가 없어 잠깐 견디다가 말씀으로 인하여 환난이나 박해가 일어나는 때에는 곧 넘어지는 자요

18 Still others, like seed sown among thorns, hear the word;
스틸 어더즈, 라익 시드 소운 어멍 쏜즈, 히어 더 워드
또 어떤 이는 가시떨기에 뿌려진 자니 이들은 말씀을 듣기는 하되

19 but the worries of this life, the deceitfulness of wealth and the desires for other things come in and choke the word, making it unfruitful.
벗 더 워이즈 어브 디스 라이프, 더 더싯펄너스 어브 웰쓰 언드 더 디자여즈 포어 어더 씽즈 컴 인 언드 초욱 더 워드, 메이킹 잇 언프룻펄.
세상의 염려와 재물의 유혹과 기타 욕심이 들어와 말씀을 막아 결실하지 못하게 되는 자요

20 Others, like seed sown on good soil, hear the word, accept it, and produce a crop—some thirty, some sixty or some a hundred times what was sown."
어더즈, 라익 시드 소운 안 구드 소일, 히어 더 워드, 억셉트 잇, 언드 프러두스 어 크랍 섬 써디, 섬 식스티 오어 섬 어 헌드러드 타임즈 윗 와즈 소운.
좋은 땅에 뿌려졌다는 것은 곧 말씀을 듣고 받아 삼십 배나 육십 배나 백 배의 결실을 하는 자니라

John 15 : 10~11

10 If you keep my commands, you will remain in my love, just as I have kept my Father's commands and

remain in his love.
이프 유 킵 마이 커맨즈, 유 윌 리메인 인 마이 러브, 저스트 애즈 아이 해브 켑트 마이 파더즈 커맨즈 언드 리메인 인 히즈 러브.
내가 아버지의 계명을 지켜 그의 사랑 안에 거하는 것 같이 너희도 내 계명을 지키면 내 사랑 안에 거하리라

11 I have told you this so that my joy may be in you and that your joy may be complete.
아이 해브 토울드 유 디스 소우 댓 마이 조이 메이 비 인 유 언드 댓 요어 조이 메이 비 컴플릿.
내가 이것을 너희에게 이름은 내 기쁨이 너희 안에 있어 너희 기쁨을 충만하게 하려 함이라

Romans 2 : 12~13

12 All who sin apart from the law will also perish apart from the law, and all who sin under the law will be judged by the law.
올 후 신 어파아트 프럼 더 로 윌 올소우 페어리쉬 어파아트 프럼 더 로, 언드 올 후 신 언더 더 로 윌 비 저지드 바이 더 로.
무릇 율법 없이 범죄한 자는 또한 율법 없이 망하고 무릇 율법이 있고 범죄한 자는 율법으로 말미암아 심판을 받으리라

13 For it is not those who hear the law who are righteous in God's sight, but it is those who obey the law who will be declared righteous.
포어 잇 이즈 낫 도우즈 후 히어 더 로 후 아아 라이처스 인 가즈 사이트, 벗 잇 이즈 도우즈 후 오우베이 더 로 후 윌 비 디클레어드 라이처스.
하나님 앞에서는 율법을 듣는 자가 의인이 아니요 오직 율법을 행하는 자라야 의롭다 하심을 얻으리니

1 Corinthians 15 : 1~2

1 Now, brothers and sisters, I want to remind you of the gospel I preached to you, which you received and on which you have taken your stand.
나우, 브러더즈 언드 시스터즈, 아이 완트 투 리마인드 유 어브 더 가스펄 아이 프리치트 투 유, 위치 유 러시브드 언드 안 위치 유 해브 테이컨 요어 스탠드.
형제들아 내가 너희에게 전한 복음을 너희에게 알게 하노니 이는 너희가 받은 것이요 또 그 가운데 선 것이라

2 By this gospel you are saved, if you hold firmly to the word I preached to you. Otherwise, you have believed in vain.
바이 디스 가스펄 유 아아 세이브드, 이프 유 호울드 펌리 투 더 워드 아이 프리치트 투 유. 어더와이즈, 유 해브 빌리브드 인 베인.
너희가 만일 내가 전한 그 말을 굳게 지키고 헛되이 믿지 아니하였으면 그로 말미암아 구원을 받으리라

1 John 2 : 3~6

3 We know that we have come to know him if we keep his commands.
위 노우 댓 위 해브 컴 투 노우 힘 이프 위 킵 히즈 커맨즈.
우리가 그의 계명을 지키면 이로써 우리가 그를 아는 줄로 알 것이요

4 Whoever says, "I know him," but does not do what he commands is a liar, and the truth is not in that person.
후에버 세즈, 아이 노우 힘, 벗 더즈 낫 두 웟 히 커맨즈 이즈 어 라이어, 언드 더 트루쓰 이즈 낫 인 댓 퍼선.
그를 아노라 하고 그의 계명을 지키지 아니하는 자는 거짓말하는 자요 진리가 그 속에 있지 아니하되

5 But if anyone obeys his word, love for God is truly made complete in them. This is how we know we are in him:
벗 이프 에니원 오우베이즈 히즈 워드, 러브 포어 가드 이즈 트룰리 메이드 컴플릿 인 뎀. 디스 이즈 하우 위 노우 위 아아 인 힘
누구든지 그의 말씀을 지키는 자는 하나님의 사랑이 참으로 그 속에서 온전하게 되었나니 이로써 우리가 그의 안에 있는 줄을 아노라

6 Whoever claims to live in him must live as Jesus did.
후에버 클레임즈 투 리브 인 힘 머스트 리브 애즈 지저스 디드.
그의 안에 산다고 하는 사는 그가 행하시는 대로 자기도 행할지니라

Revelation 1 : 1~3

1 The revelation from Jesus Christ, which God gave him to show his servants what must soon take place.
He made it known by sending his angel to his servant John,
더 레벌레이션 프럼 지저스 크라이스트, 위치 가드 게이브 힘 투 쇼우 히즈 서번트스 윗 머스트 순 테익 플레이스. 히 메이드 잇 노운 바이 센딩 히즈 에인절 투 히즈 서번트 잔,
예수 그리스도의 계시라 이는 하나님이 그에게 주사 반드시 속히 일어날 일들을 그 종들에게 보이시려고 그의 천사를 그 종 요한에게 보내어 알게 하신 것이라

2 who testifies to everything he saw—that is, the word of God and the testimony of Jesus Christ.
후 테스티파이즈 투 에브리씽 히 소 댓 이즈, 더 워드 어브 가드 언드 더 테스티모우니 어브 지저스 크라이스트.
요한은 하나님의 말씀과 예수 그리스도의 증거 곧 자기가 본 것을 다 증언하였느니라

3 Blessed is the one who reads aloud the words of this prophecy, and blessed are those who hear it and take
to heart what is written in it, because the time is near.
블레스트 이즈 더 원 후 리즈 얼라우드 더 워즈 어브 디스 프라퍼시, 언드 블레스트 아아 도우즈 후 히어 잇 언드 테익 투 하아트 윗 이즈 리턴 인 잇, 비카즈 더 타임 이즈 니어.
이 예언의 말씀을 읽는 자와 듣는 자와 그 가운데에 기록한 것을 지키는 자는 복이 있나니 때가 가까움이라

Revelation 22 : 18~21

18 I warn everyone who hears the words of the prophecy of this scroll: If anyone adds anything to them,
God will add to that person the plagues described in this scroll.
아이 원 에브리원 후 히어즈 더 워즈 어브 더 프라퍼시 어브 디스 스크로울 이프 에니원 애즈 에니씽 투 뎀, 가드 윌 애드 투 댓 퍼선 더 플레이그즈 디스크라이브드 인 디스 스크로울.
내가 이 두루마리의 예언의 말씀을 듣는 모든 사람에게 증언하노니 만일 누구든지 이것들 외에 더하면 하나님이 이 두루마리에 기록된 재앙들을 그에게 더하실 것이요

19 And if anyone takes words away from this scroll of prophecy, God will take away from that person any
share in the tree of life and in the Holy City, which are described in this scroll.
언드 이프 에니원 테익스 워즈 어웨이 프럼 디스 스크로울 어브 프라퍼시, 가드 윌 테익 어웨이 프럼 댓 퍼선 에니 셰어 인 더 트리 어브 라이프 언드 인 더 호울리 시티, 위치 아아 디스크라이브드 인 디스 스크로울.
만일 누구든지 이 두루마리의 예언의 말씀에서 제하여 버리면 하나님이 이 두루마리에 기록된 생명나무와 및 거룩한 성에 참여함을 제하여 버리시리라

20 He who testifies to these things says, "Yes, I am coming soon." Amen. Come, Lord Jesus.
히 후 테스티파이즈 투 디즈 씽즈 세즈, 예스, 아이 앰 커밍 순. 어멘. 컴, 로어드 지저스.
이것들을 증언하신 이가 이르시되 내가 진실로 속히 오리라 하시거늘 아멘 주 예수여 오시옵소서

21 The grace of the Lord Jesus be with God's people. Amen.
더 그레이스 어브 더 로어드 지저스 비 윋 가즈 피펄. 어멘.
주 예수의 은혜가 모든 자들에게 있을지어다 아멘

law [lɔː] n. 법률, 법학	directed [diréktid] a. 유도된	abolish [əbάliʃ] vt. 폐지하다
plague [pleig] n. 전염병, 페스트	observe [əbzə́ːrv] vt. 지키다	surpass [sərpǽs] vt. …보다 낫다
strike [straik] vt. 치다, 두드리다	ancestor [ǽnsestər] n. 선조, 조상	authority [əθɔ́ːriti] n. 권위, 권한
celebrate [séləbrèit] vt. 경축하다	prolong [proulɔ́ːŋ] vt. 늘이다, 오래 끌다	thorn [θɔːrn] n. 가시
ordinance [ɔ́ːrdənəns] n. 법령, 의식	submit [səbmít] vt. 복종시키다	declare [dikléər] vt. 선언하다
covenant [kʌ́vənənt] n. 계약	shun [ʃʌn] vt. 피하다	firmly [fə́ːrmli] ad. 굳게, 단단히
labor [léibər] n. 노동, 근로	overflow [òuvərflóu] vi. 넘치다	scroll [skroul] n. 두루마리

Guide them on their way. 그들의 길을 인도하시는도다

Exodus 13 : 21~22

21 By day the LORD went ahead of them in a pillar of cloud to guide them on their way and by night in a

pillar of fire to give them light, so that they could travel by day or night.
바이 데이 더 로어드 웬트 어헤드 어브 뎀 인 어 필러 어브 클라우드 투 가이드 뎀 안 데어 웨이 언드 바이 나이트 인 어 필러 어브 파여 투 기브 뎀 라이트, 소우 댓 데이 쿠드 트래벌 바이 데이 오어 나이트.
여호와께서 그들 앞에서 가시며 낮에는 구름 기둥으로 그들의 길을 인도하시고 밤에는 불 기둥을 그들에게 비추사 낮이나 밤이나 진행하게 하시니

22 Neither the pillar of cloud by day nor the pillar of fire by night left its place in front of the people.
나이더 더 필러 어브 클라우드 바이 데이 노어 더 필러 어브 파여 바이 나이트 레프트 잇스 플레이스 인 프런트 어브 더 피펄.
낮에는 구름 기둥, 밤에는 불 기둥이 백성 앞에서 떠나지 아니하니라

Psalms 23 : 1~6

1 The LORD is my shepherd, I lack nothing.
더 로어드 이즈 마이 셰퍼드, 아이 랙 너씽.
여호와는 나의 목자시니 내게 부족함이 없으리로다

2 He makes me lie down in green pastures, he leads me beside quiet waters,
히 메익스 미 라이 다운 인 그린 패스처즈, 히 리즈 미 비사이드 콰엇 워터즈,
그가 나를 푸른 풀밭에 누이시며 쉴 만한 물 가로 인도하시는도다

3 he refreshes my soul. He guides me along the right paths for his name's sake.
히 리프레쉬즈 마이 소울. 히 가이즈 미 얼롱 더 라이트 팬즈 포어 히즈 네임즈 세익.
내 영혼을 소생시키시고 자기 이름을 위하여 의의 길로 인도하시는도다

4 Even though I walk through the darkest valley, I will fear no evil, for you are with me; your rod and your staff, they comfort me.
이빈 도우 아이 웍 쓰루 더 다아커스트 밸리, 아이 윌 피어 노우 이벌, 포어 유 아아 윋 미 요어 라드 언드 요어 스태프, 데이 컴퍼트 미.
내가 사망의 음침한 골짜기로 다닐지라도 해를 두려워하지 않을 것은 주께서 나와 함께 하심이라 주의 지팡이와 막대기가 나를 안위하시나이다

5 You prepare a table before me in the presence of my enemies. You anoint my head with oil; my cup overflows.
유 프리페어 어 테이벌 비포어 미 인 더 프레전스 어브 마이 에너미즈. 유 어노인트 마이 헤드 윋 오일 마이 컵 오우버플로우즈.
주께서 내 원수의 목전에서 내게 상을 차려 주시고 기름을 내 머리에 부으셨으니 내 잔이 넘치나이다

6 Surely your goodness and love will follow me all the days of my life, and I will dwell in the house of the LORD forever.
슈얼리 요어 구드너스 언드 러브 윌 팔로우 미 올 더 데이즈 어브 마이 라이프, 언드 아이 윌 퉬 인 더 하우스 어브 더 로어드 퍼레버.
내 평생에 선하심과 인자하심이 반드시 나를 따르리니 내가 여호와의 집에 영원히 살리로다

John 10 : 14~16

14 "I am the good shepherd; I know my sheep and my sheep know me—
아이 앰 더 구드 셰퍼드 아이 노우 마이 쉽 언드 마이 쉽 노우 미
나는 선한 목자라 나는 내 양을 알고 양도 나를 아는 것이

15 just as the Father knows me and I know the Father—and I lay down my life for the sheep.
저스트 애즈 더 파더 노우즈 미 언드 아이 노우 더 파더 언드 아이 레이 다운 마이 라이프 포어 더 쉽.
아버지께서 나를 아시고 내가 아버지를 아는 것 같으니 나는 양을 위하여 목숨을 버리노라

16 I have other sheep that are not of this sheep pen. I must bring them also. They too will listen to my voice, and there shall be one flock and one shepherd.
아이 해브 어더 쉽 댓 아아 낫 어브 디스 쉽 펜. 아이 머스트 브링 뎀 올소우. 데이 투 윌 리선 투 마이 보이스, 언드 데어 섈 비 원 플락 언드 원 셰퍼드.
또 이 우리에 들지 아니한 다른 양들이 내게 있어 내가 인도하여야 할 터이니 그들도 내 음성을 듣고 한 무리가 되어 한

목자에게 있으리라

Revelation 14 : 4~5

4 These are those who did not defile themselves with women, for they remained virgins. They follow the Lamb wherever he goes. They were purchased from among mankind and offered as firstfruits to God and the Lamb.
디즈 아아 도우즈 후 디드 낫 디파일 뎀셀브즈 윋 위먼, 포어 데이 리메인드 버전즈. 데이 팔로우 더 램 웨레버 히 고우즈. 데이 워 퍼처스트 프럼 어멍 맨카인드 언드 오퍼드 애즈 퍼스트프룻스 투 가드 언드 더 램.
이 사람들은 여자와 더불어 더럽히지 아니하고 순결한 자라 어린 양이 어디로 인도하든지 따라가는 자며 사람 가운데에서 속량함을 받아 처음 익은 열매로 하나님과 어린 양에게 속한 자들이니

5 No lie was found in their mouths; they are blameless.
노우 라이 와즈 파운드 인 데어 마욷즈 데이 아아 블레임러스.
그 입에 거짓말이 없고 흠이 없는 자들이더라

ahead [əhéd] ad. 전방에, 앞에
pillar [pílər] n. 기둥
cloud [klaud] n. 구름
guide [gaid] n. 안내자
shepherd [ʃépərd] n. 양치는 사람
pasture [pǽstʃər] n. 목장
beside [bisáid] prep. …의 곁에
valley [vǽli] n. 골짜기, 유역
staff [stæf] n. 막대기, 지휘봉
prepare [pripɛ́ər] vt. 준비하다
flock [flɑk] n. 무리, 떼
goodness [gúdnis] n. 선량, 친절
dwell [dwel] vi. 살다
voice [vɔis] n. 목소리
sheep [ʃiːp] n. 양
defile [difáil] vt. 더럽히다
virgin [vəːrdʒin] n. 처녀
purchase [pəːrtʃəs] vt. 사다
offer [ɔ́(ː)fər] vt. 제공하다
firstfruits [fəːrstfruːts] n. 첫 수확
mouth [mauθ] n. 입, 식솔

The LORD watches over you. 여호와는 너를 지키시는 이시라

Psalms 121 : 1~8

1 I lift up my eyes to the mountains—where does my help come from?
아이 리프트 업 마이 아이즈 투 더 마운턴즈 웨어 더즈 마이 헬프 컴 프럼?
내가 산을 향하여 눈을 들리라 나의 도움이 어디서 올까

2 My help comes from the LORD, the Maker of heaven and earth.
마이 헬프 컴즈 프럼 더 로어드, 더 메이커 어브 헤번 언드 어쓰.
나의 도움은 천지를 지으신 여호와에게서로다

3 He will not let your foot slip—he who watches over you will not slumber;
히 윌 낫 렛 요어 풋 슬립 히 후 와처즈 오우버 유 윌 낫 슬럼버
여호와께서 너를 실족하지 아니하게 하시며 너를 지키시는 이가 졸지 아니하시리로다

4 indeed, he who watches over Israel will neither slumber nor sleep.
인디드, 히 후 와처즈 오우버 이즈리얼 윌 나이더 슬럼버 노어 슬립.
이스라엘을 지키시는 이는 졸지도 아니하시고 주무시지도 아니하시리로다

5 The LORD watches over you—the LORD is your shade at your right hand;
더 로어드 와처즈 오우버 유 더 로어드 이즈 요어 셰이드 앳 요어 라이트 핸드
여호와는 너를 지키시는 이시라 여호와께서 네 오른쪽에서 네 그늘이 되시나니

6 the sun will not harm you by day, nor the moon by night.
더 선 윌 낫 함 유 바이 데이, 노어 더 문 바이 나이트.
낮의 해가 너를 상하게 하지 아니하며 밤의 달도 너를 해치지 아니하리로다

7 The LORD will keep you from all harm—he will watch over your life;
더 로어드 윌 킵 유 프럼 올 함 히 윌 와치 오우버 요어 라이프
여호와께서 너를 지켜 모든 환난을 면하게 하시며 또 네 영혼을 지키시리로다

8 the LORD will watch over your coming and going both now and forevermore.
더 로어드 윌 와치 오우버 요어 커밍 언드 고우잉 보우쓰 나우 언드 퍼레버모어.

여호와께서 너의 출입을 지금부터 영원까지 지키시리로다

Psalms 16 : 5~11

5 LORD, you alone are my portion and my cup; you make my lot secure.
로어드, 유 얼로운 아아 마이 포어션 언드 마이 컵 유 메익 마이 랏 시큘.
여호와는 나의 산업과 나의 잔의 소득이시니 나의 분깃을 지키시나이다

6 The boundary lines have fallen for me in pleasant places; surely I have a delightful inheritance.
더 바운더리 라인즈 해브 팔런 포어 미 인 플레전트 플레이서즈 슈얼리 아이 해브 어 딜랏펄 인헤러턴스.
내게 줄로 재어 준 구역은 아름다운 곳에 있음이여 나의 기업이 실로 아름답도다

7 I will praise the LORD, who counsels me; even at night my heart instructs me.
아이 윌 프레이즈 더 로어드, 후 카운설즈 미 이빈 앳 나이트 마이 하아트 인스트럭트스 미.
나를 훈계하신 여호와를 송축할지라 밤마다 내 양심이 나를 교훈하도다

8 I keep my eyes always on the LORD. With him at my right hand, I will not be shaken.
아이 킵 마이 아이즈 올웨이즈 안 더 로어드. 윋 힘 앳 마이 라이트 핸드, 아이 윌 낫 비 셰이컨.
내가 여호와를 항상 내 앞에 모심이여 그가 나의 오른쪽에 계시므로 내가 흔들리지 아니하리로다

9 Therefore my heart is glad and my tongue rejoices; my body also will rest secure,
데어포어 마이 하아트 이즈 글래드 언드 마이 텅 리조이서즈 마이 바디 올소우 윌 레스트 시큘,
이러므로 나의 마음이 기쁘고 나의 영도 즐거워하며 내 육체도 안전히 살리니

10 because you will not abandon me to the realm of the dead, nor will you let your faithful one see decay.
비카즈 유 윌 낫 어밴던 미 투 더 렐므 어브 더 데드, 노어 윌 유 렛 요어 페이쓰펄 원 시 디케이.
이는 주께서 내 영혼을 스올에 버리지 아니하시며 주의 거룩한 자를 멸망시키지 않으실 것임이니이다

11 You make known to me the path of life; you will fill me with joy in your presence, with eternal pleasures at your right hand.
유 메익 노운 투 미 더 패쓰 어브 라이프 유 윌 필 미 윋 조이 인 요어 프레전스, 윋 이터널 플레저즈 앳 요어 라이트 핸드.
주께서 생명의 길을 내게 보이시리니 주의 앞에는 충만한 기쁨이 있고 주의 오른쪽에는 영원한 즐거움이 있나이다

mountain [máuntən] n. 산	boundary [báundəri] n. 경계, 한계	instruct [instrʌ́kt] vt. 가르치다
slip [slip] vi. 미끄러지다	portion [pɔ́ːrʃən] n. 한 조각	shake [ʃeik] vt. 흔들다
watch [watʃ] vt. 지켜보다	secure [sikjúər] a. 안전한	therefore [ðέərfɔ̀ːr] ad. 그런 까닭에
slumber [slʌ́mbər] n. 잠	delightful [diláitfəl] a. 매우 기쁜	rejoice [ridʒɔ́is] vi. 기뻐하다
indeed [indíːd] ad. 실로, 참으로	inheritance [inhéritəns] n. 상속	abandon [əbǽndən] vt. 버리다
shade [ʃeid] n. 그늘, 땅거미	praise [preiz] n. 칭찬, 숭배	realm [relm] n.왕국, 범위
harm [hɑːrm] n. 해, 손해	counsel [káunsəl] n. 의논, 조언	decay [dikéi] vi. 썩다, 쇠하다

I will answer him. 내가 그에게 응답하리라

Psalms 91 : 14~16

14 "Because he loves me," says the LORD, "I will rescue him; I will protect him, for he acknowledges my name.
비카즈 히 러브즈 미, 세즈 더 로어드, 아이 윌 레스큐 힘 아이 윌 프러텍트 힘, 포어 히 액날리지즈 마이 네임.
하나님이 이르시되 그가 나를 사랑한즉 내가 그를 건지리라 그가 내 이름을 안즉 내가 그를 높이리라

15 He will call on me, and I will answer him; I will be with him in trouble, I will deliver him and honor him.
히 윌 콜 안 미, 언드 아이 윌 앤서 힘 아이 윌 비 윋 힘 인 트러벌, 아이 윌 딜리버 힘 언드 아너 힘.
그가 내게 간구하리니 내가 그에게 응답하리라 그들이 환난 당할 때에 내가 그와 함께 하여 그를 건지고 영화롭게 하리라

16 With long life I will satisfy him and show him my salvation."
윋 롱 라이프 아이 윌 새터스파이 힘 언드 쇼우 힘 마이 샐베이션.
내가 그를 장수하게 함으로 그를 만족하게 하며 나의 구원을 그에게 보이리라 하시도다

Psalms 37 : 4~6

4 Take Delight in the LORD, and he will give you the desires of your heart.
테익 딜랏 인 더 로어드, 언드 히 윌 기브 유 더 디자여즈 어브 요어 하아트.
또 여호와를 기뻐하라 그가 네 마음의 소원을 네게 이루어 주시리로다

5 Commit your way to the LORD; trust in him and he will do this:
커밋 요어 웨이 투 더 로어드 트러스트 인 힘 언드 히 윌 두 디스
네 길을 여호와께 맡기라 그를 의지하면 그가 이루시고

6 He will make your righteous reward shine like the dawn, your vindication like the noonday sun.
히 윌 메익 요어 라이처스 리워어드 샤인 라익 더 돈, 요어 빈더케이션 라익 더 눈데이 선.
네 의를 빛 같이 나타내시며 네 공의를 정오의 빛 같이 하시리로다

Psalms 50 : 14~15

14 "Sacrifice thank offerings to God, fulfill your vows to the Most High,
새크러파이스 쌩크 오퍼링즈 투 가드, 풀필 요어 바우즈 투 더 모우스트 하이,
감사로 하나님께 제사를 드리며 지존하신 이에게 네 서원을 갚으며

15 and call on me in the day of trouble; I will deliver you, and you will honor me."
언드 콜 안 미 인 더 데이 어브 트러벌 아이 윌 딜리버 유, 언드 유 윌 아너 미.
환난 날에 나를 부르라 내가 너를 건지리니 네가 나를 영화롭게 하리로다

Psalms 145 : 18~20

18 The LORD is near to all who call on him, to all who call on him in truth.
더 로어드 이즈 니어 투 올 후 콜 안 힘, 투 올 후 콜 안 힘 인 트루쓰.
여호와께서는 자기에게 간구하는 모든 자 곧 진실하게 간구하는 모든 자에게 가까이 하시는도다

19 He fulfills the desires of those who fear him; he hears their cry and saves them.
히 풀필즈 더 디자여즈 어브 도우즈 후 피어 힘 히 히어즈 데어 크라이 언드 세이브즈 뎀.
그는 자기를 경외하는 자들의 소원을 이루시며 또 그들의 부르짖음을 들으사 구원하시리로다

20 The LORD watches over all who love him, but all the wicked he will destroy.
더 로어드 와처즈 오우버 올 후 러브 힘, 벗 올 더 위커드 히 윌 디스트로이.
여호와께서 자기를 사랑하는 자들은 다 보호하시고 악인들은 다 멸하시리로다

Isaiah 30 : 18~19

18 Yet the LORD longs to be gracious to you; therefore he will rise up to show you compassion. For the LORD is a God of justice. Blessed are all who wait for him!
옛 더 로어드 롱즈 투 비 그레이셔스 투 유 데어포어 히 윌 라이즈 업 투 쇼우 유 컴패션. 포어 더 로어드 이즈 어 가드 어브 저스터스. 블레스트 아아 올 후 웨잇 포어 힘!
그러나 여호와께서 기다리시나니 이는 너희에게 은혜를 베풀려 하심이요 일어나시리니 이는 너희를 긍휼히 여기려 하심이라 대저 여호와는 정의의 하나님이심이라 그를 기다리는 자마다 복이 있도다

19 People of Zion, who live in Jerusalem, you will weep no more. How gracious he will be when you cry for help! As soon as he hears, he will answer you.
피펄 어브 자이언, 후 라이브 인 저루설럼, 유 윌 윕 노우 모어. 하우 그레이셔스 히 윌 비 웬 유 크라이 포어 헬프! 애즈 순 애즈 히 히어즈, 히 윌 앤서 유.
시온에 거주하며 예루살렘에 거주하는 백성아 너는 다시 통곡하지 아니할 것이라 그가 네 부르짖는 소리로 말미암아 네게 은혜를 베푸시되 그가 들으실 때에 네게 응답하시리라

Jeremiah 33 : 2~3

2 "This is what the LORD says, he who made the earth, the LORD who formed it and established it—the LORD is his name:
디스 이즈 윗 더 로어드 세즈, 히 후 메이드 디 어쓰, 더 로어드 후 폼드 잇 언드 이스태블리쉬트 잇 더 로어드 이즈 히즈 네임
일을 행하시는 여호와, 그것을 만들며 성취하시는 여호와, 그의 이름을 여호와라 하는 이가 이와 같이 이르시도다

3 'Call to me and I will answer you and tell you great and unsearchable things you do not know.'
콜 투 미 언드 아이 윌 앤서 유 언드 텔 유 그레이트 언드 언서처벌 씽즈 유 두 낫 노우.
너는 내게 부르짖으라 내가 네게 응답하겠고 네가 알지 못하는 크고 은밀한 일을 네게 보이리라

Matthew 6 : 9~13

9 "This, then, is how you should pray: " 'Our Father in heaven, hallowed be your name,
디스, 덴, 이즈 하우 유 슈드 프레이 아우어 파더 인 헤번, 핼로우드 비 요어 네임,
그러므로 너희는 이렇게 기도하라 하늘에 계신 우리 아버지여 이름이 거룩히 여김을 받으시오며

10 your kingdom come, your will be done, on earth as it is in heaven.
요어 킹덤 컴, 요어 윌 비 던, 안 어쓰 애즈 잇 이즈 인 헤번.
나라가 임하시오며 뜻이 하늘에서 이루어진 것 같이 땅에서도 이루어지이다

11 Give us today our daily bread.
기브 어스 터데이 아우어 데일리 브레드.
오늘 우리에게 일용할 양식을 주시옵고

12 And forgive us our debts, as we also have forgiven our debtors.
언드 퍼기브 어스 아우어 뎃스, 애즈 위 올소우 해브 퍼기번 아우어 데터즈.
우리가 우리에게 죄 지은 자를 사하여 준 것 같이 우리 죄를 사하여 주시옵고

13 And lead us not into temptation, but deliver us from the evil one. (for yours is the kingdom and the
power and the glory forever. Amen.)'
언드 리드 어스 낫 인투 템테이션, 벗 딜리버 어스 프럼 디 이벌 원. (포어 유어즈 이즈 더 킹덤 언드 더 파워 언드 더 글로
어리 퍼레버. 어멘.)
우리를 시험에 들게 하지 마시옵고 다만 악에서 구하시옵소서 (나라와 권세와 영광이 아버지께 영원히 있사옵나이다 아멘)

Mark 11 : 22~24

22 "Have faith in God," Jesus answered.
해브 페이쓰 인 가드, 지저스 앤서드.
예수께서 그들에게 대답하여 이르시되 하나님을 믿으라

23 "Truly I tell you, if anyone says to this mountain, 'Go, throw yourself into the sea,' and does not doubt
in their heart but believes that what they says will happen, it will be done for them.
트룰리 아이 텔 유, 이프 에니원 세즈 투 디스 마운턴, 고우, 쓰로우 요어셀프 인투 더 시, 언드 더즈 낫 다우트 인 데어 하
아트 벗 빌리브즈 댓 웟 데이 세즈 윌 해펀, 잇 윌 비 던 포어 뎀.
내가 진실로 너희에게 이르노니 누구든지 이 산더러 들리어 바다에 던져지라 하며 그 말하는 것이 이루어질 줄 믿고 마
음에 의심하지 아니하면 그대로 되리라

24 Therefore I tell you, whatever you ask for in prayer, believe that you have received it, and it will be yours.
데어포어 아이 텔 유, 워테버 유 애스크 포어 인 프레어, 빌리브 댓 유 해브 러시브드 잇, 언드 잇 윌 비 유어즈.
그러므로 내가 너희에게 말하노니 무엇이든지 기도하고 구하는 것은 받은 줄로 믿으라 그리하면 너희에게 그대로 되리라

John 14 : 12~14

12 Very truly I tell you, whoever believes in me will do the works I have been doing, and they will do even
greater things than these, because I am going to the Father.
베어리 트룰리 아이 텔 유, 후에버 빌리브즈 인 미 윌 두 더 웍스 아이 해브 빈 두잉, 언드 데이 윌 두 이빈 그레이터 씽즈
던 디즈, 비카즈 아이 앰 고우잉 투 디 파더.
내가 진실로 진실로 너희에게 이르노니 나를 믿는 자는 내가 하는 일을 그도 할 것이요 또한 그보다 큰 일도 하리니 이는
내가 아버지께로 감이라

13 And I will do whatever you ask in my name, so that the Father may be glorified in the Son.
언드 아이 윌 두 워테버 유 애스크 인 마이 네임, 소우 댓 더 파더 메이 비 글로어러파이드 인 더 선.
너희가 내 이름으로 무엇을 구하든지 내가 행하리니 이는 아버지로 하여금 아들로 말미암아 영광을 받으시게 하려 함이라

14 You may ask me for anything in my name, and I will do it.

유 메이 애스크 미 포어 에니씽 인 마이 네임, 언드 아이 윌 두 잇.
내 이름으로 무엇이든지 내게 구하면 내가 행하리라

John 16 : 23~24

23 In that day you will no longer ask me anything. Very truly I tell you, my Father will give you whatever you ask in my name.
인 댓 데이 유 윌 노우 롱거 애스크 미 에니씽. 베어리 트룰리 아이 텔 유, 마이 파더 윌 기브 유 워테버 유 애스크 인 마이 네임.
그 날에는 너희가 아무 것도 내게 묻지 아니하리라 내가 진실로 진실로 너희에게 이르노니 너희가 무엇이든지 아버지께 구하는 것을 내 이름으로 주시리라

24 Until now you have not asked for anything in my name. Ask and you will receive, and your joy will be complete.
언틸 나우 유 해브 낫 애스크트 포어 에니씽 인 마이 네임. 애스크 언드 유 윌 러시브, 언드 요어 조이 윌 비 컴플릿.
지금까지는 너희가 내 이름으로 아무 것도 구하지 아니하였으나 구하라 그리하면 받으리니 너희 기쁨이 충만하리라

Philippians 4 : 6~7

6 Do not be anxious about anything, but in every situation, by prayer and petition, with thanksgiving, present your requests to God.
두 낫 비 앵크셔스 어바우트 에니씽, 벗 인 에브리 시추에이션, 바이 프레어 언드 퍼티션, 윋 쌩크스기빙, 프리젠트 요어 리퀘스트스 투 가드.
아무 것도 염려하지 말고 다만 모든 일에 기도와 간구로, 너희 구할 것을 감사함으로 하나님께 아뢰라

7 And the peace of God, which transcends all understanding, will guard your hearts and your minds in Christ Jesus.
언드 더 피스 어브 가드, 위치 트랜센즈 올 언더스탠딩, 윌 가아드 요어 하아트스 언드 요어 마인즈 인 크라이스트 지저스.
그리하면 모든 지각에 뛰어난 하나님의 평강이 그리스도 예수 안에서 너희 마음과 생각을 지키시리라

1 Thessalonians 5 : 16~18

16 Rejoice always;
리조이스 올웨이즈
항상 기뻐하라

17 pray continually;
프레이 컨티뉴얼리
쉬지 말고 기도하라

18 give thanks in all circumstances; for this is God's will for you in Christ Jesus.
기브 쌩크스 인 올 서컴스탠서즈 포어 디스 이즈 가즈 윌 포어 유 인 크라이스트 지저스.
범사에 감사하라 이것이 그리스도 예수 안에서 너희를 향하신 하나님의 뜻이니라

1 Timothy 4 : 4~5

4 For everything God created is good, and nothing is to be rejected if it is received with thanksgiving,
포어 에브리씽 가드 크리에이터드 이즈 구드, 언드 너씽 이즈 투 비 리젝티드 이프 잇 이즈 러시브드 윋 쌩크스기빙,
하나님께서 지으신 모든 것이 선하매 감사함으로 받으면 버릴 것이 없나니

5 because it is consecrated by the word of God and prayer.
비카즈 잇 이즈 칸서크레이터드 바이 더 워드 어브 가드 언드 프레어.
하나님의 말씀과 기도로 거룩하여짐이라

James 1 : 2~5

2 Consider it pure joy, my brothers and sisters, whenever you face trials of many kinds,
컨시더 잇 퓨 조이, 마이 브러더즈 언드 시스터즈, 웨네버 유 페이스 트라열즈 어브 메니 카인즈,
내 형제들아 너희가 여러 가지 시험을 당하거든 온전히 기쁘게 여기라

3 because you know that the testing of your faith produces perseverance.

비카즈 유 노우 댓 더 테스팅 어브 요어 페이쓰 프러두서즈 퍼서비런스.
이는 너희 믿음의 시련이 인내를 만들어 내는 줄 너희가 앎이라

4 Let perseverance finish its work so that you may be mature and complete, not lacking anything.
렛 퍼서비런스 피니쉬 잇스 웍 소우 댓 유 메이 비 머추어 언드 컴플릿, 낫 래킹 에니씽.
인내를 온전히 이루라 이는 너희로 온전하고 구비하여 조금도 부족함이 없게 하려 함이라

5 If any of you lacks wisdom, you should ask God, who gives generously to all without finding fault, and it will be given to you.
이프 에니 어브 유 랙스 위즈덤, 유 슈드 애스크 가드, 후 기브즈 제너러슬리 투 올 위다우트 파인딩 폴트, 언드 잇 윌 비 기번 투 유.
너희 중에 누구든지 지혜가 부족하거든 모든 사람에게 후히 주시고 꾸짖지 아니하시는 하나님께 구하라 그리하면 주시리라

1 John 5 : 13~15

13 I write these things to you who believe in the name of the Son of God so that you may know that you have eternal life.
아이 라이트 디즈 씽즈 투 유 후 빌리브 인 더 네임 어브 더 선 어브 가드 소우 댓 유 메이 노우 댓 유 해브 이터널 라이프.
내가 하나님의 아들의 이름을 믿는 너희에게 이것을 쓰는 것은 너희로 하여금 너희에게 영생이 있음을 알게 하려 함이라

14 This is the confidence we have in approaching God: that if we ask anything according to his will, he hears us.
디스 이즈 더 칸퍼덴스 위 해브 인 업로우칭 가드 댓 이프 위 애스크 에니씽 어코어딩 투 히즈 윌, 히 히어즈 어스.
그를 향하여 우리가 가진 바 담대함이 이것이니 그의 뜻대로 무엇을 구하면 들으심이라

15 And if we know that he hears us—whatever we ask—we know that we have what we asked of him.
언드 이프 위 노우 댓 히 히어즈 어스 워테버 위 애스크 위 노우 댓 위 해브 웟 위 애스크트 어브 힘.
우리가 무엇이든지 구하는 바를 들으시는 줄을 안즉 우리가 그에게 구한 그것을 얻은 줄을 또한 아느니라

rescue [réskjuː] vt. 구조하다	desire [dizáiər] vt. 바라다, 원하다	establish [istǽbliʃ] vt. 설립하다
protect [prətékt] vt. 보호하다	vindication [vìndəkéiʃən] n. 옹호	hallow [hǽlou] vt. 신에게 바치다
acknowledge [æknɑ́lidʒ-] vt. 인정하다	offering [ɔ́(ː)fəriŋ] n. 공물, 헌금	complete [kəmplíːt] a. 완전한
trouble [trʌ́bəl] n 고생, 두통	fulfill [fulfíl] vt. 이행하다, 완료하다	situation [sìtʃuéiʃən] n. 위치, 입장
deliver [dilívər] vt. 인도하다	fear [fiər] n. 두려움, 근심	petition [pitíʃən] n. 청원, 청원서
satisfy [sǽtisfài] vt. 충족시키다	compassion [kəmpǽʃən] n. 동정	circumstance [sə́ːrkəmstæ̀ns] n. 상황
salvation [sælvéiʃən] n. 구조, 구제	form [fɔːrm] n. 모양, 형식	confidence [kɑ́nfidəns] n. 신용

Good fruit. 아름다운 열매

Matthew 7 : 17~20

17 Likewise, every good tree bears good fruit, but a bad tree bears bad fruit.
라이콰즈, 에브리 구드 트리 베어즈 구드 프룻, 벗 어 배드 트리 베어즈 배드 프룻.
이와 같이 좋은 나무마다 아름다운 열매를 맺고 못된 나무가 나쁜 열매를 맺나니

18 A good tree cannot bear bad fruit, and a bad tree cannot bear good fruit.
어 구드 트리 캐낫 베어 배드 프룻, 언드 어 배드 트리 캐낫 베어 구드 프룻.
좋은 나무가 나쁜 열매를 맺을 수 없고 못된 나무가 아름다운 열매를 맺을 수 없느니라

19 Every tree that does not bear good fruit is cut down and thrown into the fire.
에브리 트리 댓 더즈 낫 베어 구드 프룻 이즈 컷 다운 언드 쓰로운 인투 더 파여.
아름다운 열매를 맺지 아니하는 나무마다 찍혀 불에 던져지느니라

20 Thus, by their fruit you will recognize them.
더스, 바이 데어 프룻 유 윌 레커그나이즈 뎀.
이러므로 그들의 열매로 그들을 알리라

Genesis 2 : 15~17

15 The LORD God took the man and put him in the Garden of Eden to work it and take care of it.
더 로어드 가드 툭 더 맨 언드 풋 힘 인 더 가아던 어브 이던 투 웍 잇 언드 테익 케어 어브 잇.
여호와 하나님이 그 사람을 이끌어 에덴 동산에 두어 그것을 경작하며 지키게 하시고

16 And the LORD God commanded the man, "You are free to eat from any tree in the garden;
언드 더 로어드 가드 커맨디드 더 맨, 유 아아 프리 투 잇 프럼 에니 트리 인 더 가아던
여호와 하나님이 그 사람에게 명하여 이르시되 동산 각종 나무의 열매는 네가 임의로 먹되

17 but you must not eat from the tree of the knowledge of good and evil, for when you eat from it you will certainly die."
벗 유 머스트 낫 잇 프럼 더 트리 어브 더 날러지 어브 구드 언드 이벌, 포어 웬 유 잇 프럼 잇 유 윌 서터늘리 다이.
선악을 알게 하는 나무의 열매는 먹지 말라 네가 먹는 날에는 반드시 죽으리라 하시니라

John 15 : 1~8

1 "I am the true vine, and my Father is the gardener.
아이 앰 더 트루 바인, 언드 마이 파더 이즈 더 가아더너.
나는 참 포도나무요 내 아버지는 농부라

2 He cuts off every branch in me that bears no fruit, while every branch that does bear fruit he prunes so that it will be even more fruitful.
히 컷스 오프 에브리 브랜치 인 미 댓 베어즈 노우 프룻, 와일 에브리 브랜치 댓 더즈 베어 프룻 히 프룬즈 소우 댓 잇 윌 비 이빈 모어 프룻펄.
무릇 내게 붙어 있어 열매를 맺지 아니하는 가지는 아버지께서 그것을 제거해 버리시고 무릇 열매를 맺는 가지는 더 열매를 맺게 하려 하여 그것을 깨끗하게 하시느니라

3 You are already clean because of the word I have spoken to you.
유 아아 올레디 클린 비카즈 어브 더 워드 아이 해브 스포우컨 투 유.
너희는 내가 일러준 말로 이미 깨끗하여졌으니

4 Remain in me, as I also remain in you. No branch can bear fruit by itself; it must remain in the vine. Neither can you bear fruit unless you remain in me.
리메인 인 미, 애즈 아이 올소우 리메인 인 유. 노우 브랜치 캔 베어 프룻 바이 잇셀프 잇 머스트 리메인 인 더 바인. 나이더 캔 유 베어 프룻 언레스 유 리메인 인 미.
내 안에 거하라 나도 너희 안에 거하리라 가지가 포도나무에 붙어 있지 아니하면 스스로 열매를 맺을 수 없음 같이 너희도 내 안에 있지 아니하면 그러하리라

5 "I am the vine; you are the branches. If you remain in me and I in you, you will bear much fruit; apart from me you can do nothing.
아이 앰 더 바인 유 아아 더 브랜처즈. 이프 유 리메인 인 미 언드 아이 인 유, 유 윌 베어 머치 프룻 어파아트 프럼 미 유 캔 두 너씽.
나는 포도나무요 너희는 가지라 그가 내 안에, 내가 그 안에 거하면 사람이 열매를 많이 맺나니 나를 떠나서는 너희가 아무 것도 할 수 없음이라

6 If you do not remain in me, you are like a branch that is thrown away and withers; such branches are picked up, thrown into the fire and burned.
이프 유 두 낫 리메인 인 미, 유 아아 라익 어 브랜치 댓 이즈 쓰로운 어웨이 언드 위더즈 서치 브랜처즈 아아 픽트 업, 쓰로운 인투 더 파여 언드 번드.
사람이 내 안에 거하지 아니하면 가지처럼 밖에 버려져 마르나니 사람들이 그것을 모아다가 불에 던져 사르느니라

7 If you remain in me and my words remain in you, ask whatever you wish, and it will be done for you.
이프 유 리메인 인 미 언드 마이 워즈 리메인 인 유, 애스크 워테버 유 위쉬, 언드 잇 윌 비 던 포어 유.
너희가 내 안에 거하고 내 말이 너희 안에 거하면 무엇이든지 원하는 대로 구하라 그리하면 이루리라

8 This is to my Father's glory, that you bear much fruit, showing yourselves to be my disciples.
디스 이즈 투 마이 파더즈 글로어리, 댓 유 베어 머치 프룻, 쇼우잉 유어셀브즈 투 비 마이 디사이펄즈.

너희가 열매를 많이 맺으면 내 아버지께서 영광을 받으실 것이요 너희는 내 제자가 되리라

1 Corinthians 14 : 12~15

12 So it is with you. Since you are eager for gifts of the Spirit, try to excel in those that build up the church.
소우 잇 이즈 윋 유. 신스 유 아아 이거 포어 기프트스 어브 더 스피럿, 트라이 투 익셀 인 도우즈 댓 빌드 업 더 처치.
그러므로 너희도 영적인 것을 사모하는 자인즉 교회의 덕을 세우기 위하여 그것이 풍성하기를 구하라

13 For this reason the one who speaks in a tongue should pray that they may interpret what they say.
포어 디스 리전 더 원 후 스픽스 인 어 텅 슈드 프레이 댓 데이 메이 인털럿 웟 데이 세이.
그러므로 방언을 말하는 자는 통역하기를 기도할지니

14 For if I pray in a tongue, my spirit prays, but my mind is unfruitful.
포어 이프 아이 프레이 인 어 텅, 마이 스피럿 프레이즈, 벗 마이 마인드 이즈 언프룻펄.
내가 만일 방언으로 기도하면 나의 영이 기도하거니와 나의 마음은 열매를 맺지 못하리라

15 So what shall I do? I will pray with my spirit, but I will also pray with my understanding; I will sing with my spirit, but I will also sing with my understanding.
소우 웟 섈 아이 두? 아이 윌 프레이 윋 마이 스피럿, 벗 아이 윌 올소우 프레이 윋 마이 언더스탠딩 아이 윌 싱 윋 마이 스피럿, 벗 아이 윌 올소우 싱 윋 마이 언더스탠딩.
그러면 어떻게 할까 내가 영으로 기도하고 또 마음으로 기도하며 내가 영으로 찬송하고 또 마음으로 찬송하리라

Galatians 5 : 22~23

22 But the fruit of the Spirit is love, joy, peace, forbearance, kindness, goodness, faithfulness,
벗 더 프룻 어브 더 스피럿 이즈 러브, 조이, 피스, 포어베런스, 카인드너스, 구드너스, 페이쓰펄네스,
오직 성령의 열매는 사랑과 희락과 화평과 오래 참음과 자비와 양선과 충성과

23 gentleness and self-control. Against such things there is no law.
젠털너스 언드 셀프컨트로울. 어겐스트 서치 씽즈 데어 이즈 노우 로.
온유와 절제니 이같은 것을 금지할 법이 없느니라

Ephesians 5 : 8~9

8 For you were once darkness, but now you are light in the Lord. Live as children of light
포어 유 워 원스 다아크너스, 벗 나우 유 아아 라이트 인 더 로어드. 라이브 애즈 칠드런 어브 라이트
너희가 전에는 어둠이더니 이제는 주 안에서 빛이라 빛의 자녀들처럼 행하라

9 (for the fruit of the light consists in all goodness, righteousness and truth)
(포어 더 프룻 어브 더 라이트 컨시스트스 인 올 구드너스, 라이처스너스 언드 트루쓰)
빛의 열매는 모든 착함과 의로움과 진실함에 있느니라

James 3 : 17~18

17 But the wisdom that comes from heaven is first of all pure; then peace-loving, considerate, submissive, full of mercy and good fruit, impartial and sincere.
벗 더 위즈덤 댓 컴즈 프럼 헤번 이즈 퍼스트 어브 올 퓰 덴 피스러빙, 컨시더럿, 서브미시브, 풀 어브 머시 언드 구드 프룻, 임파아셜 언드 신시어.
오직 위로부터 난 지혜는 첫째 성결하고 다음에 화평하고 관용하고 양순하며 긍휼과 선한 열매가 가득하고 편견과 거짓이 없나니

18 Peacemakers who sow in peace reap a harvest of righteousness.
피스메이커즈 후 사우 인 피스 립 어 하아버스트 어브 라이처스너스.
화평하게 하는 자들은 화평으로 심어 의의 열매를 거두느니라

2 Peter 1 : 5~11

5 For this very reason, make every effort to add to your faith goodness; and to goodness, knowledge;
포어 디스 베어리 리전, 메익 에브리 에퍼트 투 애드 투 요어 페이쓰 구드너스 언드 투 구드너스, 날러지
그러므로 너희가 더욱 힘써 너희 믿음에 덕을, 덕에 지식을,

6 and to knowledge, self-control; and to self-control, perseverance; and to perseverance, godliness;

언드 투 날러지, 셀프컨트로울 언드 투 셀프컨트로울, 퍼서비런스 언드 투 퍼서비런스, 가들리너스
지식에 절제를, 절제에 인내를, 인내에 경건을,

7 and to godliness, mutual affection; and to mutual affection, love.
언드 투 가들리너스, 뮤추얼 어펙션 언드 투 뮤추얼 어펙션, 러브.
경건에 형제 우애를, 형제 우애에 사랑을 더하라

8 For if you possess these qualities in increasing measure, they will keep you from being ineffective and unproductive in your knowledge of our Lord Jesus Christ.
포어 이프 유 퍼제스 디즈 콸러티즈 인 인크리싱 메저, 데이 윌 킵 유 프럼 비잉 이니펙티브 언드 언프러덕티브 인 요어 날러지 어브 아우어 로어드 지저스 크라이스트.
이런 것이 너희에게 있어 흡족한즉 너희로 우리 주 예수 그리스도를 알기에 게으르지 않고 열매 없는 자가 되지 않게 하려니와

9 But whoever does not have them is nearsighted and blind, forgetting that they have been cleansed from their past sins.
벗 후에버 더즈 낫 해브 뎀 이즈 니어사이티드 언드 블라인드, 퍼게팅 댓 데이 해브 빈 클렌즈드 프럼 데어 패스트 신즈.
이런 것이 없는 자는 맹인이라 멀리 보지 못하고 그의 옛 죄가 깨끗하게 된 것을 잊었느니라

10 Therefore, my brothers and sisters, make every effect to confirm your calling and election. For if you do these things, you will never stumble,
데어포어, 마이 브러더즈 언드 시스터즈, 메익 에브리 이펙트 투 컨펌 요어 콜링 언드 일렉션. 포어 이프 유 두 디즈 씽즈, 유 윌 네버 스텀벌,
그러므로 형제들아 더욱 힘써 너희 부르심과 택하심을 굳게 하라 너희가 이것을 행한즉 언제든지 실족하지 아니하리라

11 and you will receive a rich welcome into the eternal kingdom of our Lord and Savior Jesus Christ.
언드 유 윌 러시브 어 리치 웰컴 인투 디 이터널 킹덤 어브 아우어 로어드 언드 세이브여 지저스 크라이스트.
이같이 하면 우리 주 곧 구주 예수 그리스도의 영원한 나라에 들어감을 넉넉히 너희에게 주시리라

Revelation 22 : 1~2

1 Then the angel showed me the river of the water of life, as clear as crystal, flowing from the throne of God and of the Lamb
덴 디 에인절 쇼우드 미 더 리버 어브 더 워터 어브 라이프, 애즈 클리어 애즈 크리스털, 플로우잉 프럼 더 쓰로운 어브 가드 언드 어브 더 램
또 그가 수정 같이 맑은 생명수의 강을 내게 보이니 하나님과 및 어린 양의 보좌로부터 나와서

2 down the middle of the great street of the city. On each side of the river stood the tree of life, bearing twelve crops of fruit, yielding its fruit every month. And the leaves of the tree are for the healing of the nations.
다운 더 미덜 어브 더 그레이트 스트릿 어브 더 시티. 안 이치 사이드 어브 더 리버 스투드 더 트리 어브 라이프, 베링 트웰브 크랍스 어브 프룻, 일딩 잇스 프룻 에브리 먼쓰. 언드 더 리브즈 어브 더 트리 아아 포어 더 힐링 어브 더 네이션즈.
길 가운데로 흐르더라 강 좌우에 생명나무가 있어 열두 가지 열매를 맺되 달마다 그 열매를 맺고 그 나무 잎사귀들은 만국을 치료하기 위하여 있더라

likewise [láikwàiz] ad. 똑같이, 또한
bear [bɛər] vt. 나르다
recognize [rékəgnàiz] vt. 알아보다
command [kəmǽnd] vt. …에게 명하다
certainly [sə́:rtənli] ad. 확실히
gardenerr [gɑ́:rdnər] n. 정원사
branch [bræntʃ] n. 가지, 파생물

prune [pru:n] vt. 잘라내다
throw [θrou] vt. 던지다
wither [wíðər] vi. 시들다, 쇠퇴하다
excel [iksél] vt. 능가하다
forbearance [fɔ:rbɛ́ərəns] n. 인내
gentleness [dʒéntlnis] n. 온순, 친절
consist [kənsíst] vi. 되다

considerate [kənsídərit] a. 동정심 많은
submissive [səbmísiv] a. 복종하는
impartial [impɑ́:rʃəl] a. 공평한
sincere [sinsíər] a. 성실한
mutual [mjú:tʃuəl] a. 서로의, 공동의
measure [méʒər] vt. 재다
nearsight [niərsait] n. 근시

To do the will of him who sent me. 나를 보내신 이의 뜻을 행하려 함이니라

John 6 : 38~40

38 For I have come down from heaven not to do my will but to do the will of him who sent me.
포어 아이 해브 컴 다운 프럼 헤번 낫 투 두 마이 윌 벗 투 두 더 윌 어브 힘 후 센트 미.
내가 하늘에서 내려온 것은 내 뜻을 행하려 함이 아니요 나를 보내신 이의 뜻을 행하려 함이니라

39 And this is the will of him who sent me, that I shall lose none of all those he has given me, but raise them up at the last day.
언드 디스 이즈 더 윌 어브 힘 후 센트 미, 댓 아이 섈 루즈 넌 어브 올 도우즈 히 해즈 기번 미, 벗 레이즈 뎀 업 앳 더 래스트 데이.
나를 보내신 이의 뜻은 내게 주신 자 중에 내가 하나도 잃어버리지 아니하고 마지막 날에 다시 살리는 이것이니라

40 For my Father's will is that everyone who looks to the Son and believes in him shall have eternal life, and I will raise them up at the last day."
포어 마이 파더즈 윌 이즈 댓 에브리원 후 룩스 투 더 선 언드 빌리브즈 인 힘 섈 해브 이터널 라이프, 언드 아이 윌 레이즈 뎀 업 앳 더 래스트 데이.
내 아버지의 뜻은 아들을 보고 믿는 자마다 영생을 얻는 이것이니 마지막 날에 내가 이를 다시 살리리라 하시니라

Matthew 7 : 21

21 "Not everyone who says to me, 'Lord, Lord,' will enter the kingdom of heaven, but only the one who does the will of my Father who is in heaven.
낫 에브리원 후 세즈 투 미, 로어드, 로어드, 윌 엔터 더 킹덤 어브 헤번, 벗 오운리 더 원 후 더즈 더 윌 어브 마이 파더 후 이즈 인 헤번.
나더러 주여 주여 하는 자마다 다 천국에 들어갈 것이 아니요 다만 하늘에 계신 내 아버지의 뜻대로 행하는 자라야 들어가리라

Matthew 12 : 49~50

49 Pointing to his disciples, he said, "Here are my mother and my brothers.
포인팅 투 히즈 디사이펄즈, 히 세드, 히어 아아 마이 머더 언드 마이 브러더즈.
손을 내밀어 제자들을 가리켜 이르시되 나의 어머니와 나의 동생들을 보라

50 For whoever does the will of my Father in heaven is my brother and sister and mother."
포어 후에버 더즈 더 윌 어브 마이 파더 인 헤번 이즈 마이 브러더 언드 시스터 언드 머더.
누구든지 하늘에 계신 내 아버지의 뜻대로 하는 자가 내 형제요 자매요 어머니이니라 하시더라

Luke 22 : 42~43

42 "Father, if you are willing, take this cup from me; yet not my will, but yours be done."
파더, 이프 유 아아 윌링, 테익 디스 컵 프럼 미 옛 낫 마이 윌, 벗 유어즈 비 던.
이르시되 아버지여 만일 아버지의 뜻이거든 이 잔을 내게서 옮기시옵소서 그러나 내 원대로 마시옵고 아버지의 원대로 되기를 원하나이다 하시니

43 An angel from heaven appeared to him and strengthened him.
앤 에인절 프럼 헤번 어피어드 투 힘 언드 스트렝썬드 힘.
천사가 하늘로부터 예수께 나타나 힘을 더하더라

come [kʌm] vi. 오다
down [daun] ad. 아래
will [wil] n. 의지
send [send] vt. 보내다, 발송하다
shall [ʃæl] v. …일 것이다
lose [lu:z] vt. 잃다, 놓쳐버리다
raise [reiz] vt. 올리다, 끌어올리다
believe [bilí:v] vt. 믿다, 신용하다
eternal [itə́:rnəl] a. 영원한, 끝없는
everyone [évriwʌ̀n] pron. 모든 사람
lord [lɔ:rd] n. 지배자, 주
enter [éntər] vt. …에 들어가다
kingdom [kíŋdəm] n. 왕국, 왕토
heaven [hévən] n. 하늘, 천국
only [óunli] a. 유일한, …만의
pointing ['pɔɪntɪŋ] n. 뾰족하게 함, 지적
disciple [disáipəl] n. 제자, 문하생
here [hiər] ad. 여기
take [teik] vt. 손에 잡다, 쥐다
appear [əpíər] vi. 나타나다, …로 보이다
strengthen [stréŋkθən] vt. 강하게 하다

All people to be saved. 모든 사람이 구원을 받으며

1 Timothy 2 : 3~6

3 This is good, and pleases God our Savior,
디스 이즈 구드 언드 플리지즈 가드 아우어 세이브여,
이것이 우리 구주 하나님 앞에 선하고 받으실 만한 것이니,
4 who wants all people to be saved and to come to a knowledge of the truth.
후 완트스 올 피펄 투 비 세이브드 언드 투 컴 투 어 날러지 어브 더 트루쓰.
하나님은 모든 사람이 구원을 받으며 진리를 아는 데에 이르기를 원하시느니라
5 For there is one God and one mediator between God and mankind, the man Christ Jesus,
포어 데어 이즈 원 가드 언드 원 미디에이터 비트윈 가드 언드 맨카인드, 더 맨 크라이스트 지저스,
하나님은 한 분이시요 또 하나님과 사람 사이에 중보자도 한 분이시니 곧 사람이신 그리스도 예수라
6 who gave himself as a ransom for all people. This has now been witnessed to at the proper time.
후 게이브 힘셀프 애즈 어 랜섬 포어 올 피펄. 디스 해즈 나우 빈 윗너스트 투 앳 더 프라퍼 타임.
그가 모든 사람을 위하여 자기를 대속물로 주셨으니 기약이 이르러 주신 증거니라

Matthew 19 : 25~26

25 When the disciples heard this, they were greatly astonished and asked, "Who then can be saved?"
웬 더 디사이펄즈 허드 디스, 데이 워 그레잇리 어스타니쉬트 언드 애스크트, 후 덴 캔 비 세이브드?
제자들이 듣고 몹시 놀라 이르되 그렇다면 누가 구원을 얻을 수 있으리이까
26 Jesus looked at them and said, "With man this is impossible, but with God all things are possible."
지저스 룩트 앳 뎀 언드 세드, 윋 맨 디스 이즈 임파서벌, 벗 윋 가드 올 씽즈 아아 파서벌.
예수께서 그들을 보시며 이르시되 사람으로는 할 수 없으나 하나님으로서는 다 하실 수 있느니라

Mark 8 : 34~35

34 Then he called the crowd to him along with his disciples and said: "Whoever wants to be my disciple must deny themselves and take up their cross and follow me.
덴 히 콜드 더 크라우드 투 힘 얼롱 윋 히즈 디사이펄즈 언드 세드 후에버 완트스 투 비 마이 디사이펄 머스트 디나이 뎀셀브즈 언드 테익 업 데어 크로스 언드 팔로우 미.
무리와 제자들을 불러 이르시되 누구든지 나를 따라오려거든 자기를 부인하고 자기 십자가를 지고 나를 따를 것이니라
35 For whoever wants to save their life will lose it, but whoever loses their life for me and for the gospel will save it.
포어 후에버 완트스 투 세이브 데어 라이프 윌 루즈 잇, 벗 후에버 루지즈 데어 라이프 포어 미 언드 포어 더 가스펄 윌 세이브 잇.
누구든지 자기 목숨을 구원하고자 하면 잃을 것이요 누구든지 나와 복음을 위하여 자기 목숨을 잃으면 구원하리라

Mark 16 : 15~16

15 He said to them, "Go into all the world and preach the gospel to all creation.
히 세드 투 뎀, 고우 인투 올 더 월드 언드 프리치 더 가스펄 투 올 크리에이션.
또 이르시되 너희는 온 천하에 다니며 만민에게 복음을 전파하라
16 Whoever believes and is baptized will be saved, but whoever does not believe will be condemned.
후에버 빌리브즈 언드 이즈 뱁타이즈드 윌 비 세이브드, 벗 후에버 더즈 낫 빌리브 윌 비 컨뎀드.
믿고 세례를 받는 사람은 구원을 얻을 것이요 믿지 않는 사람은 정죄를 받으리라

Colossians 2 : 13~15

13 When you were dead in your sins and in the uncircumcision of your flesh, God made you alive with Christ. He forgave us all our sins,
웬 유 워 데드 인 요어 신즈 언드 인 디 언서컴시전 어브 요어 플레쉬, 가드 메이드 유 얼라이브 윋 크라이스트. 히 퍼게이브 어스 올 아우어 신즈,
또 범죄와 육체의 무할례로 죽었던 너희를 하나님이 그와 함께 살리시고 우리의 모든 죄를 사하시고
14 having canceled the charge of our legal indebtedness, which stood against us and condemned us; he has

taken it away, nailing it to the cross.
해빙 캔설드 더 차아지 어브 아우어 리걸 인데티드니스, 위치 스투드 어겐스트 어스 언드 컨뎀드 어스 히 해즈 테이컨 잇 어웨이, 네일링 잇 투 더 크로스.
우리를 거스르고 불리하게 하는 법조문으로 쓴 증서를 지우시고 제하여 버리사 십자가에 못 박으시고

15 And having disarmed the powers and authorities, he made a public spectacle of them, triumphing over them by the cross.
언드 해빙 디삼드 더 파워즈 언드 어쏘러티즈, 히 메이드 어 퍼블릭 스펙터컬 어브 뎀, 트라이엄핑 오우버 뎀 바이 더 크로스.
통치자들과 권세들을 무력화하여 드러내어 구경거리로 삼으시고 십자가로 그들을 이기셨느니라

2 Timothy 3 : 14~17

14 But as for you, continue in what you have learned and have become convinced of, because you know those from whom you learned it,
벗 애즈 포어 유, 컨티뉴 인 왓 유 해브 런드 언드 해브 비컴 컨빈스트 어브, 비카즈 유 노우 도우즈 프럼 훔 유 런드 잇,
그러나 너는 배우고 확신한 일에 거하라 너는 네가 누구에게서 배운 것을 알며

15 and how from infancy you have known the Holy Scriptures, which are able to make you wise for salvation through faith in Christ Jesus.
언드 하우 프럼 인펀시 유 해브 노운 더 호울리 스크립처즈, 위치 아아 에이벌 투 메익 유 와이즈 포어 샐베이션 쓰루 페이쓰 인 크라이스트 지저스.
또 어려서부터 성경을 알았나니 성경은 능히 너로 하여금 그리스도 예수 안에 있는 믿음으로 말미암아 구원에 이르는 지혜가 있게 하느니라

16 All Scripture is God-breathed and is useful for teaching, rebuking, correcting and training in righteousness,
올 스크립처 이즈 가드브릳드 언드 이즈 유스펄 포어 티칭, 리뷰킹, 커렉팅 언드 트레이닝 인 라이처스너스,
모든 성경은 하나님의 감동으로 된 것으로 교훈과 책망과 바르게 함과 의로 교육하기에 유익하니

17 so that the servant of God may be thoroughly equipped for every good work.
소우 댓 더 서번트 어브 가드 메이 비 써로우리 이퀍트 포어 에브리 구드 웍.
이는 하나님의 사람으로 온전하게 하며 모든 선한 일을 행할 능력을 갖추게 하려 함이라

mediator [míːdièitər] n. 조정자, 중재인	creation [kriːéiʃən] n. 창조, 창조물	nail [neil] n. 손톱, 못
knowledge [nálidʒ] n. 지식	baptize [bæptáiz] vi. 세례를 주다	disarm [disáːrm] vt. 무장 해제하다
ransom [rǽnsəm] n. 몸값, 속전	condemn [kəndém] vt. 비난하다	authority [əθɔ́ːriti] n. 권위, 권한
astonish [əstániʃ] vt. 놀라게 하다	flesh [fleʃ] n. 살	spectacle [spéktəkəl] n. 광경, 구경거리
possible [pásəbəl] a. 가능한	forgive [fərgív] vt. 용서하다, 탕감하다	triumph [tráiəmf] n. 승리, 대성공
deny [dinái] vt. 부정하다, 거부하다	cancel [kǽnsəl] vt. …을 지우다	infancy [ínfənsi] n. 어릴 때, 유아
gospel [gáspəl] n. 복음, 복음서	legal [líːgəl] a. 법률의, 법정의	equip [ikwíp] vt. 갖추다

God is love. 하나님은 사랑이심이라

1 John 4 : 7~9

7 Dear friends, let us love one another, for love comes from God. Everyone who loves has been born of God and knows God.
디어 프렌즈, 렛 어스 러브 원 어너더, 포어 러브 컴즈 프럼 가드. 에브리원 후 러브즈 해즈 빈 본 어브 가드 언드 노우즈 가드.
사랑하는 자들아 우리가 서로 사랑하자 사랑은 하나님께 속한 것이니 사랑하는 자마다 하나님으로부터 나서 하나님을 알고

8 Whoever does not love does not know God, because God is love.
후에버 더즈 낫 러브 더즈 낫 노우 가드, 비카즈 가드 이즈 러브.
사랑하지 아니하는 자는 하나님을 알지 못하나니 이는 하나님은 사랑이심이라

9 This is how God showed his love among us: He sent his one and only Son into the world that we might live through him.
디스 이즈 하우 가드 쇼우드 히즈 러브 어멍 어스 히 센트 히즈 원 언드 오운리 선 인투 더 월드 댓 위 마이트 리브 쓰루 힘.

하나님의 사랑이 우리에게 이렇게 나타난 바 되었으니 하나님이 자기의 독생자를 세상에 보내심은 그로 말미암아 우리를 살리려 하심이라

Mark 12 : 29~31

29 "The most important one," answered Jesus, "is this: 'Hear, O Israel: the Lord our God, the Lord is one.
더 모우스트 임포어턴트 원, 앤서드 지저스, 이즈 디스 히어, 오우 이즈리얼 더 로어드 아우어 가드, 더 로어드 이즈 원.
예수께서 대답하시되 첫째는 이것이니 이스라엘아 들으라 주 곧 우리 하나님은 유일한 주시라

30 Love the Lord your God with all your heart and with all your soul and with all your mind and with all your strength.'
러브 더 로어드 요어 가드 윋 올 요어 하아트 언드 윋 올 요어 소울 언드 윋 올 요어 마인드 언드 윋 올 요어 스트렝쓰.
네 마음을 다하고 목숨을 다하고 뜻을 다하고 힘을 다하여 주 너의 하나님을 사랑하라 하신 것이요

31 The second is this: 'Love your neighbor as yourself.' There is no commandment greater than these."
더 세컨드 이즈 디스 러브 요어 네이버 애즈 요어셀프. 데어 이즈 노우 커맨드먼트 그레이터 던 디즈.
둘째는 이것이니 네 이웃을 네 자신과 같이 사랑하라 하신 것이라 이보다 더 큰 계명이 없느니라

Luke 11 : 42

42 "Woe to you Pharisees, because you give God a tenth of your mint, rue and all other kinds of garden herbs, but you neglect justice and the love of God. You should have practiced the latter without leaving the former undone.
워우 투 유 패어리시즈, 비카즈 유 기브 가드 어 텐쓰 어브 요어 민트, 루 언드 올 어더 카인즈 어브 가아던 어브즈, 벗 유 너글렉트 저스터스 언드 더 러브 어브 가드. 유 슈드 해브 프랙티스트 더 래터 위다우트 리빙 더 포어머 언던.
화 있을진저 너희 바리새인이여 너희가 박하와 운향과 모든 채소의 십일조는 드리되 공의와 하나님께 대한 사랑은 버리는도다 그러나 이것도 행하고 저것도 버리지 말아야 할지니라

John 3 : 16~17

16 For God so loved the world that he gave his one and only Son, that whoever believes in him shall not perish but have eternal life.
포어 가드 소우 러브드 더 월드 댓 히 게이브 히즈 원 언드 오운리 선, 댓 후에버 빌리브즈 인 힘 섈 낫 페어리쉬 벗 해브 이터널 라이프.
하나님이 세상을 이처럼 사랑하사 독생자를 주셨으니 이는 그를 믿는 자마다 멸망하지 않고 영생을 얻게 하려 하심이라

17 For God did not send his Son into the world to condemn the world, but to save the world through him.
포어 가드 디드 낫 센드 히즈 선 인투 더 월드 투 컨뎀 더 월드, 벗 투 세이브 더 월드 쓰루 힘.
하나님이 그 아들을 세상에 보내신 것은 세상을 심판하려 하심이 아니요 그로 말미암아 세상이 구원을 받게 하려 하심이라

John 13 : 34~35

34 "A new command I give you: Love one another. As I have loved you, so you must love one another.
어 누 커맨드 아이 기브 유 러브 원 어너더. 애즈 아이 해브 러브드 유, 소우 유 머스트 러브 원 어너더.
새 계명을 너희에게 주노니 서로 사랑하라 내가 너희를 사랑한 것 같이 너희도 서로 사랑하라

35 By this everyone will know that you are my disciples, if you love one another."
바이 디스 에브리원 윌 노우 댓 유 아아 마이 디사이펄즈, 이프 유 러브 원 어너더.
너희가 서로 사랑하면 이로써 모든 사람이 너희가 내 제자인 줄 알리라

Ephesians 4 : 11~15

11 So Christ himself gave the apostles, the prophets, the evangelists, the pastors and teachers,
소우 크라이스트 힘셀프 게이브 디 어포설즈, 더 프라펏스, 디 이밴절리스트스, 더 패스터즈 언드 티처즈,
그가 어떤 사람은 사도로, 어떤 사람은 선지자로, 어떤 사람은 복음 전하는 자로, 어떤 사람은 목사와 교사로 삼으셨으니

12 to equip his people for works of service, so that the body of Christ may be built up
투 이큅 히즈 피펄 포어 웍스 어브 서버스, 소우 댓 더 바디 어브 크라이스트 메이 비 빌트 업
이는 성도를 온전하게 하여 봉사의 일을 하게 하며 그리스도의 몸을 세우려 하심이라

13 until we all reach unity in the faith and in the knowledge of the Son of God and become mature, attaining

to the whole measure of the fullness of Christ.
언틸 위 올 리치 유너티 인 더 페이쓰 언드 인 더 날러지 어브 더 선 어브 가드 언드 비컴 머추어, 어테이닝 투 더 호울 메저 어브 더 풀너스 어브 크라이스트.
우리가 다 하나님의 아들을 믿는 것과 아는 일에 하나가 되어 온전한 사람을 이루어 그리스도의 장성한 분량이 충만한 데까지 이르리니

14 Then we will no longer be infants, tossed back and forth by the waves, and blown here and there by every wind of teaching and by the cunning and craftiness of people in their deceitful scheming.
덴 위 윌 노우 롱거 비 인펀트스, 토스트 백 언드 포어쓰 바이 더 웨이브즈, 언드 블로운 히어 언드 데어 바이 에브리 윈드 어브 티칭 언드 바이 더 커닝 언드 크래프티너스 어브 피펄 인 데어 디싯펄 스키밍.
이는 우리가 이제부터 어린 아이가 되지 아니하여 사람의 속임수와 간사한 유혹에 빠져 온갖 교훈의 풍조에 밀려 요동하지 않게 하려 함이라

15 Instead, speaking the truth in love, we will grow to become in every respect the mature body of him who is the head, that is, Christ.
인스테드, 스피킹 더 트루쓰 인 러브, 위 윌 그로우 투 비컴 인 에브리 리스펙트 더 머추어 바디 어브 힘 후 이즈 더 헤드, 댓 이즈, 크라이스트.
오직 사랑 안에서 참된 것을 하여 범사에 그에게까지 자랄지라 그는 머리니 곧 그리스도라

1 Peter 4 : 7~10

7 The end of all things is near. Therefore be alert and of sober mind so that you may pray.
디 엔드 어브 올 씽즈 이즈 니어. 데어포어 비 어러트 언드 어브 소우버 마인드 소우 댓 유 메이 프레이.
만물의 마지막이 가까이 왔으니 그러므로 너희는 정신을 차리고 근신하여 기도하라

8 Above all, love each other deeply, because love covers over a multitude of sins.
어버브 올, 러브 이치 어더 디플리, 비카즈 러브 커버즈 오우버 어 멀터투드 어브 신즈.
무엇보다도 뜨겁게 서로 사랑할지니 사랑은 허다한 죄를 덮느니라

9 Offer hospitality to one another without grumbling.
오퍼 하스퍼탤러티 투 원 어너더 위다우트 그럼벌링.
서로 대접하기를 원망 없이 하고

10 Each of you should use whatever gift you have received to serve others, as faithful stewards of God's grace in its various forms.
이치 어브 유 슈드 유즈 워테버 기프트 유 해브 러시브드 투 서브 어더즈, 애즈 페이쓰펄 스투어즈 어브 가즈 그레이스 인 잇스 베어리어스 폼즈.
각각 은사를 받은 대로 하나님의 여러 가지 은혜를 맡은 선한 청지기 같이 서로 봉사하라

1 John 3 : 8~10

8 The one who does what is sinful is of the devil, because the devil has been sinning from the beginning. The reason the Son of God appeared was to destroy the devil's work.
더 원 후 더즈 웟 이즈 신펄 이즈 어브 더 데벌, 비카즈 더 데벌 해즈 빈 시닝 프럼 더 비기닝. 더 리전 더 선 어브 가드 어피어드 와즈 투 디스트로 이 더 데벌즈 웍.
죄를 짓는 자는 마귀에게 속하나니 마귀는 처음부터 범죄함이라 하나님의 아들이 나타나신 것은 마귀의 일을 멸하려 하심이라

9 No one who is born of God will continue to sin, because God's seed remains in them; they cannot go on sinning, because they have been born of God.
노우 원 후 이즈 본 어브 가드 윌 컨티뉴 투 신, 비카즈 가즈 시드 리메인즈 인 뎀 데이 캐낫 고우 안 시닝, 비카즈 데이 해브 빈 본 어브 가드.
하나님께로부터 난 자마다 죄를 짓지 아니하나니 이는 하나님의 씨가 그의 속에 거함이요 그도 범죄하지 못하는 것은 하나님께로부터 났음이라

10 This is how we know who the children of God are and who the children of the devil are: Anyone who does not do what is right is not God's child, nor is anyone who does not love their brother and sister.

디스 이즈 하우 위 노우 후 더 칠드런 어브 가드 아아 언드 후 더 칠드런 어브 더 데벌 아아 에니원 후 더즈 낫 두 윗 이즈 라이트 이즈 낫 가즈 차일드, 노어 이즈 에니원 후 더즈 낫 러브 데어 브러더 언드 시스터.
이러므로 하나님의 자녀들과 마귀의 자녀들이 드러나나니 무릇 의를 행하지 아니하는 자나 또는 그 형제를 사랑하지 아니하는 자는 하나님께 속하지 아니하니라

1 John 5 : 1~4

1 Everyone who believes that Jesus is the Christ is born of God, and everyone who loves the father loves his child as well.
에브리원 후 빌리브즈 댓 지저스 이즈 더 크라이스트 이즈 본 어브 가드, 언드 에브리원 후 러브즈 더 파더 러브즈 히즈 차일드 애즈 웰.
예수께서 그리스도이심을 믿는 자마다 하나님께로부터 난 자니 또한 낳으신 이를 사랑하는 자마다 그에게서 난 자를 사랑하느니라

2 This is how we know that we love the children of God: by loving God and carrying out his commands.
디스 이즈 하우 위 노우 댓 위 러브 더 칠드런 어브 가드 바이 러빙 가드 언드 캐어리잉 아웃 히즈 커멘즈.
우리가 하나님을 사랑하고 그의 계명들을 지킬 때에 이로써 우리가 하나님의 자녀를 사랑하는 줄을 아느니라

3 In fact, this is love for God: to keep his commands. And his commands are not burdensome,
인 팩트, 디스 이즈 러브 포어 가드 투 킵 히즈 커맨즈. 언드 히즈 커맨즈 아아 낫 버던섬,
하나님을 사랑하는 것은 이것이니 우리가 그의 계명들을 지키는 것이라 그의 계명들은 무거운 것이 아니로다

4 for everyone born of God overcomes the world. This is the victory that has overcome the world, even our faith.
포어 에브리원 본 어브 가드 오우버컴즈 더 월드. 디스 이즈 더 빅터어리 댓 해즈 오우버컴 더 월드, 이빈 아우어 페이쓰.
무릇 하나님께로부터 난 자마다 세상을 이기느니라 세상을 이기는 승리는 이것이니 우리의 믿음이니라

dear [diər] a. 친애하는, 귀중한	neglect [niglékt] vt. 게을리하다	unity [jú:nəti] n. 통일, 조화
important [impɔ́:rtənt] a. 중요한	practice [prǽktis] n. 실행, 실시	mature [mətjúər] a. 익은, 심사숙고한
answer [ǽnsər] n. 대답, 해답	undone [ʌndʌ́n] a. 풀어진, 파멸한	attain [ətéin] vt. 이르다, 도달하다
neighbor [néibər] n. 이웃	perish [périʃ] vi. 멸망하다	toss [tɔ:s] vt. 던지다
commandment [kəmǽndmənt] n. 율법	condemn [kəndém] vt. 비난하다	cunning [kʌ́niŋ] a. 교활한, 잘된
mint [mint] n. 박하	apostle [əpɑ́sl] n. 사도	deceitful [disí:tfəl] a. 사람을 속이는
rue [ru:] n. 비탄, 후회	evangelist [ɪ'vændʒəlɪst] n. 전도사	steward [stjú:ərd] n. 집사, 청지기

When the Holy Spirit comes on you. 오직 성령이 너희에게 임하시면

Acts 1 : 8~9

8 But you will receive power when the Holy Spirit comes on you; and you will be my witnesses in Jerusalem, and in all Judea and Samaria, and to the ends of the earth."
벗 유 윌 러시브 파워 웬 더 호울리 스피릿 컴즈 안 유 언드 유 윌 비 마이 윗너서즈 인 저루설럼, 언드 인 올 주디어 언드 세이머리어, 언드 투 디 엔즈 어브 디 어쓰.
오직 성령이 너희에게 임하시면 너희가 권능을 받고 예루살렘과 온 유대와 사마리아와 땅 끝까지 이르러 내 증인이 되리라 하시니라

9 After he said this, he was taken up before their very eyes, and a cloud hid him from their sight.
애프터 히 세드 디스, 히 와즈 테이컨 업 비포어 데어 베어리 아이즈, 언드 어 클라우드 히 드 힘 프럼 데어 사이트.
이 말씀을 마치시고 그들이 보는데 올려져 가시니 구름이 그를 가리어 보이지 않게 하더라

Ezekiel 36 : 26~28

26 I will give you a new heart and put a new spirit in you; I will remove from you your heart of stone and give you a heart of flesh.
아이 윌 기브 유 어 누 하아트 언드 풋 어 누 스피릿 인 유 아이 윌 리무브 프럼 유 요어 하아트 어브 스토운 언드 기브 유 어 하아트 어브 플레쉬.
또 새 영을 너희 속에 두고 새 마음을 너희에게 주되 너희 육신에서 굳은 마음을 제거하고 부드러운 마음을 줄 것이며

27 And I will put my Spirit in you and move you to follow my decrees and be careful to keep my laws.
언드 아이 윌 풋 마이 스피럿 인 유 언드 무브 유 투 팔로우 마이 디크리즈 언드 비 케어펄 투 킵 마이 로즈.
또 내 영을 너희 속에 두어 너희로 내 율례를 행하게 하리니 너희가 내 규례를 지켜 행할지라
28 Then You will live in the land I gave your ancestors; you will be my people, and I will be your God.
덴 유 윌 리브 인 더 랜드 아이 게이브 요어 앤세스터즈 유 윌 비 마이 피펄, 언드 아이 윌 비 요어 가드.
28 내가 너희 조상들에게 준 땅에서 너희가 거주하면서 내 백성이 되고 나는 너희 하나님이 되리라

Joel 2 : 28~30

28 "And afterward, I will pour out my Spirit on all people. Your sons and daughters will prophesy, your old
men will dream dreams, your young men will see visions.
언드 애프터워드, 아이 윌 포어 아웃 마이 스피럿 안 올 피펄. 요어 선즈 언드 도터즈 윌 프라퍼시, 요어 오울드 멘 윌 드림 드림즈, 요어 영 멘 윌 시 비전즈.
그 후에 내가 내 영을 만민에게 부어 주리니 너희 자녀들이 장래 일을 말할 것이며 너희 늙은이는 꿈을 꾸며 너희 젊은이는 이상을 볼 것이며
29 Even on my servants, both men and women, I will pour out my Spirit in those days.
이빈 안 마이 서번트스, 보우쓰 멘 언드 위먼, 아이 윌 포어 아웃 마이 스피럿 인 도우즈 데이즈.
그 때에 내가 또 내 영을 남종과 여종에게 부어 줄 것이며
30 I will show wonders in the heavens and on the earth, blood and fire and billows of smoke.
아이 윌 쇼우 원더즈 인 더 헤번즈 언드 안 디 어쓰, 블러드 언드 파여 언드 빌로우즈 어브 스모욱.
내가 이적을 하늘과 땅에 베풀리니 곧 피와 불과 연기 기둥이라

John 4 : 23~24

23 Yet a time is coming and has now come when the true worshipers will worship the Father in the Spirit
and in truth, for they are the kind of worshipers the Father seeks.
옛 어 타임 이즈 커밍 언드 해즈 나우 컴 웬 더 트루 워쉬퍼즈 윌 워셥 더 파더 인 더 스피럿 언드 인 트루쓰, 포어 데이 아아 더 카인드 어브 워쉬퍼즈 더 파더 식스.
아버지께 참되게 예배하는 자들은 영과 진리로 예배할 때가 오나니 곧 이 때라 아버지께서는 자기에게 이렇게 예배하는 자들을 찾으시느니라
24 God is spirit, and his worshipers must worship in the Spirit and in truth."
가드 이즈 스피럿, 언드 히즈 워쉬퍼즈 머스트 워셥 인 더 스피럿 언드 트루쓰.
하나님은 영이시니 예배하는 자가 영과 진리로 예배할지니라

John 16 : 13~15

13 But when he, the Spirit of truth, comes, he will guide you into all the truth. He will not speak on his
own; he will speak only what he hears, and he will tell you what is yet to come.
벗 웬 히, 더 스피럿 어브 트루쓰, 컴즈, 히 윌 가이드 유 인투 올 더 트루쓰. 히 윌 낫 스픽 안 히즈 오운 히 윌 스픽 오운리 웟 히 히어즈, 언드 히 윌 텔 유 웟 이즈 옛 투 컴.
그러나 진리의 성령이 오시면 그가 너희를 모든 진리 가운데로 인도하시리니 그가 스스로 말하지 않고 오직 들은 것을 말하며 장래 일을 너희에게 알리시리라
14 He will glorify me because it is from me that he will receive what he will make known to you.
히 윌 글로어러파이 미 비카즈 잇 이즈 프럼 미 댓 히 윌 러시브 웟 히 윌 메익 노운 투 유.
그가 내 영광을 나타내리니 내 것을 가지고 너희에게 알리시겠음이라
15 All that belongs to the Father is mine. That is why I said the Spirit will receive from me what he will
make known to you.
올 댓 빌롱즈 투 더 파더 이즈 마인. 댓 이즈 와이 아이 세드 더 스피럿 윌 러시브 프럼 미 웟 히 윌 메익 노운 투 유.
무릇 아버지께 있는 것은 다 내 것이라 그러므로 내가 말하기를 그가 내 것을 가지고 너희에게 알리시리라 하였노라

Romans 8 : 14~15

14 For those who are led by the Spirit of God are the children of God.
포어 도우즈 후 아아 레드 바이 더 스피럿 어브 가드 아아 더 칠드런 어브 가드.

무릇 하나님의 영으로 인도함을 받는 사람은 곧 하나님의 아들이라

15 The Spirit you received does not make you slaves, so that you live in fear again; rather, the Spirit you received brought about your adoption to sonship. And by him we cry, "Abba, Father."
더 스피럿 유 러시브드 더즈 낫 메익 유 슬레이브즈, 소우 댓 유 라이브 인 피어 어겐 래더,더 스피럿 유 러시브드 브롯 어바우트 요어 어답션 투 산쉽. 언드 바이 힘 위 크라이, 애버, 파더.
너희는 다시 무서워하는 종의 영을 받지 아니하고 양자의 영을 받았으므로 우리가 아빠 아버지라고 부르짖느니라

Romans 14 : 17~18

17 For the kingdom of God is not a matter of eating and drinking, but of righteousness, peace and joy in the Holy Spirit,
포어 더 킹덤 어브 가드 이즈 낫 어 매터 어브 이팅 언드 드링킹, 벗 어브 라이처스너스, 피스 언드 조이 인 더 호울리 스피럿,
하나님의 나라는 먹는 것과 마시는 것이 아니요 오직 성령 안에 있는 의와 평강과 희락이라

18 because anyone who serves Christ in this way is pleasing to God and receives human approval.
비카즈 에니원 후 서브즈 크라이스트 인 디스 웨이 이즈 플리징 투 가드 언드 러시브즈 휴먼 업루벌.
이로써 그리스도를 섬기는 자는 하나님을 기쁘시게 하며 사람에게도 칭찬을 받느니라

1 Corinthians 2 : 10~12

10 these are the things God has revealed to us by his Spirit. The Spirit searches all things, even the deep things of God.
디즈 아아 더 씽즈 가드 해즈 리빌드 투 어스 바이 히즈 스피럿. 더 스피럿 서치즈 올 씽즈, 이빈 더 딥 씽즈 어브 가드.
오직 하나님이 성령으로 이것을 우리에게 보이셨으니 성령은 모든 것 곧 하나님의 깊은 것까지도 통달하시느니라

11 For who knows a person's thoughts except their own spirit within them? In the same way no one knows the thoughts of God except the Spirit of God.
포어 후 노우즈 어 퍼선즈 쏫스 익셉트 데어 오운 스피럿 위씬 뎀? 인 더 세임 웨이 노우 원 노우즈 더 쏫스 어브 가드 익셉트 더 스피럿 어브 가드.
사람의 일을 사람의 속에 있는 영 외에 누가 알리요 이와 같이 하나님의 일도 하나님의 영 외에는 아무도 알지 못하느니라

12 What we have received is not the spirit of the world, but the Spirit who is from God, so that we may understand what God has freely given us.
웟 위 해브 러시브드 이즈 낫 더 스피럿 어브 더 월드, 벗 더 스피럿 후 이즈 프럼 가드, 소우 댓 위 메이 언더스탠드 웟 가드 해즈 프릴리 기번 어스.
우리가 세상의 영을 받지 아니하고 오직 하나님으로부터 온 영을 받았으니 이는 우리로 하여금 하나님께서 우리에게 은혜로 주신 것들을 알게 하려 하심이라

1 Corinthians 6 : 19~20

19 Do you not know that your bodies are temples of the Holy Spirit, who is in you, whom you have received from God? You are not your own;
두 유 낫 노우 댓 요어 바디즈 아아 템펄즈 어브 더 호울리 스피럿, 후 이즈 인 유, 훔 유 해브 러시브드 프럼 가드? 유 아아 낫 요어 오운
너희 몸은 너희가 하나님께로부터 받은 바 너희 가운데 계신 성령의 전인 줄을 알지 못하느냐 너희는 너희 자신의 것이 아니라

20 you were bought at a price. Therefore honor God with your bodies.
유 워 밧 앳 어 프라이스. 데어포어 아너 가드 윋 요어 바디즈.
값으로 산 것이 되었으니 그런즉 너희 몸으로 하나님께 영광을 돌리라

Galatians 6 : 6~8

6 Nevertheless, the one who receives instruction in the word should share all good things with their instructor.
네버덜레스, 더 원 후 러시브즈 인스트럭션 인 더 워드 슈드 셰어 올 구드 씽즈 윋 데어 인스트럭터.
가르침을 받는 자는 말씀을 가르치는 자와 모든 좋은 것을 함께 하라

7 Do not be deceived: God cannot be mocked. A man reaps what he sows.

두 낫 비 디시브드 가드 캐낫 비 막트. 어 맨 립스 윗 히 소우즈.
스스로 속이지 말라 하나님은 업신여김을 받지 아니하시나니 사람이 무엇으로 심든지 그대로 거두리라

8 Whoever sows to please their flesh, from the flesh will reap destruction; whoever sows to please the Spirit, from the Spirit will reap eternal life.
후에버 소우즈 투 플리즈 데어 플레쉬, 프럼 더 플레쉬 윌 립 디스트럭션 후에버 소우즈 투 플리즈 더 스피럿, 프럼 더 스피럿 윌 립 이터널 라이프.
자기의 육체를 위하여 심는 자는 육체로부터 썩어질 것을 거두고 성령을 위하여 심는 자는 성령으로부터 영생을 거두리라

receive [risíːv] vt. 받다, 수령하다	forefather [fɔ́ːrfɑ̀ːðər] n. 조상, 선조	approval [əprúːvəl] n. 승인, 인가
power [páuər] n. 힘, 능력	afterward [ǽftərwərd] ad. 그 후	reveal [rivíːl] vt. 드러내다, 알리다
witness [wítnis] n. 증언, 증인	pour [pɔːr] vt. 따르다, 쏟다	temple [témpəl] n. 성전
sight [sait] n. 시각, 조망	billow [bílou] n. 큰 물결, 놀	price [prais] n. 가격, 대가
spirit [spírit] n. 정신, 영	slave [sleiv] n. 노예	mock [mɑk] vt. 조롱하다, 놀리다
remove [rimúːv] vt. …을 제거하다	adoption [ə'dɑːpʃn] n. 입양, 채용	sow [sou] vt. 뿌리다
decree [dikríː] n. 법령, 포고	sonship [sʌ́nʃip] n. 자식의 신	reap [riːp] vt. 베어들이다, 거둬들이다

It is finished. 이르시되 다 이루었다

John 19 : 28~30

28 Later, knowing that everything had now been finished, and so that Scripture would be fulfilled, Jesus said, "I am thirsty."
레이터, 노우잉 댓 에브리씽 해드 나우 빈 피니쉬트, 언드 소우 댓 스크립처 워드 비 풀필드, 지저스 세드, 아이 앰 써스티.
그 후에 예수께서 모든 일이 이미 이루어진 줄 아시고 성경을 응하게 하려 하사 이르시되 내가 목마르다 하시니

29 A jar of wine vinegar was there, so they soaked a sponge in it, put the sponge on a stalk of the hyssop plant, and lifted it to Jesus' lips.
어 자아 어브 와인 비너거 와즈 데어, 소우 데이 소욱트 어 스펀지 인 잇, 풋 더 스펀지 안 어 스톡 어브 더 히섭 플랜트, 언드 리프터드 잇 투 지저스 립스.
거기 신 포도주가 가득히 담긴 그릇이 있는지라 사람들이 신 포도주를 적신 해면을 우슬초에 매어 예수의 입에 대니

30 When he had received the drink, Jesus said, "It is finished." With that, he bowed his head and gave up his spirit.
웬 히 해드 러시브드 더 드링크, 지저스 세드, 잇 이즈 피니쉬트. 윋 댓, 히 바우드 히즈 헤드 언드 게이브 업 히즈 스피럿.
예수께서 신 포도주를 받으신 후에 이르시되 다 이루었다 하시고 머리를 숙이니 영혼이 떠나가시니라

Genesis 18 : 18~19

18 Abraham will surely become a great and powerful nation, and all nations on earth will be blessed through him.
에이브러햄 윌 슈얼리 비컴 어 그레이트 언드 파워펄 네이션, 언드 올 네이션즈 안 어쓰 윌 비 블레스트 쓰루 힘.
아브라함은 강대한 나라가 되고 천하 만민은 그로 말미암아 복을 받게 될 것이 아니냐

19 For I have chosen him, so that he will direct his children and his household after him to keep the way of the LORD by doing what is right and just, so that the LORD will bring about for Abraham what he has promised him."
포어 아이 해브 초우전 힘, 소우 댓 히 윌 더렉트 히즈 칠드런 언드 히즈 하우스호울드 애프터 힘 투 킵 더 웨이 어브 더 로어드 바이 두잉 윗 이즈 라이트 언드 저스트, 소우 댓 더 로어드 윌 브링 어바우트 포어 에이브러햄 윗 히 해즈 프라머스트 힘.
내가 그로 그 자식과 권속에게 명하여 여호와의 도를 지켜 공의와 정의를 행하게 하려고 그를 택하였나니 이는 나 여호와가 아브라함에게 대하여 말한 일을 이루려 함이니라

Exodus 2 : 24~25

24 God heard their groaning and he remembered his covenant with Abraham, with Isaac and with Jacob.

가드 허드 데어 그로우닝 언드 히 리멤버드 히즈 커버넌트 윋 에이브러햄, 윋 아이적 언드 윋 제이커브.
하나님이 그들의 고통 소리를 들으시고 하나님이 아브라함과 이삭과 야곱에게 세운 그의 언약을 기억하사
25 So God looked on the Israelites and was concerned about them.
소우 가드 룩트 안 디 이즈럴랏스 언드 와즈 컨선드 어바우트 뎀.
하나님이 이스라엘 자손을 돌보셨고 하나님이 그들을 기억하셨더라

Joshua 21 : 43~45

43 So the LORD gave Israel all the land he had sworn to give their ancestors, and they took possession of it and settled there.
소우 더 로어드 게이브 이즈리얼 올 더 랜드 히 해드 스원 투 기브 데어 앤세스터즈, 언드 데이 툭 퍼제션 어브 잇 언드 세털드 데어.
여호와께서 이스라엘의 조상들에게 맹세하사 주리라 하신 온 땅을 이와 같이 이스라엘에게 다 주셨으므로 그들이 그것을 차지하여 거기에 거주하였으니
44 The LORD gave them rest on every side, just as he had sworn to their ancestors. Not one of their enemies withstood them; the LORD gave all their enemies into them their hands.
더 로어드 게이브 뎀 레스트 안 에브리 사이드, 저스트 애즈 히 해드 스원 투 데어 앤세스터즈. 낫 원 어브 데어 에너미즈 위쓰스투드 뎀 더 로어드 게이브 올 데어 에너미즈 인투 뎀 데어 핸즈.
여호와께서 그들의 주위에 안식을 주셨으되 그 조상들에게 맹세하신 대로 하셨으므로 그들의 모든 원수들 중에 그들과 맞선 자가 하나도 없었으니 이는 여호와께서 그들의 모든 원수들을 그들의 손에 넘겨 주셨음이니라
45 Not one of all the LORD's good promises to Israel failed; every one was fulfilled.
낫 원 어브 올 더 로어즈 구드 프라머서즈 투 이즈리얼 페일드 에브리 원 와즈 풀필드.
여호와께서 이스라엘 족속에게 말씀하신 선한 말씀이 하나도 남음이 없이 다 응하였더라

Matthew 1 : 21~23

21 She will give birth to a son, and you are to give him the name Jesus, because he will save his people from their sins."
쉬 윌 기브 버쓰 투 어 선, 언드 유 아아 투 기브 힘 더 네임 지저스, 비카즈 히 윌 세이브 히즈 피펄 프럼 데어 신즈.
아들을 낳으리니 이름을 예수라 하라 이는 그가 자기 백성을 그들의 죄에서 구원할 자이심이라 하니라
22 All this took place to fulfill what the Lord had said through the prophet:
올 디스 툭 플레이스 투 풀필 윗 더 로어드 해드 세드 쓰루 더 프라펏
이 모든 일이 된 것은 주께서 선지자로 하신 말씀을 이루려 하심이니 이르시되
23 "The virgin will conceive and give birth to a son, and they will call him Immanuel" (which means "God with us").
더 버진 윌 컨시브 언드 기브 버쓰 투 어 선, 언드 데이 윌 콜 힘 이머눌 (위치 민즈 가드 윋 어스).
보라 처녀가 잉태하여 아들을 낳을 것이요 그의 이름은 임마누엘이라 하리라 하셨으니 이를 번역한즉 하나님이 우리와 함께 계시다 함이라

Matthew 24 : 35~36

35 Heaven and earth will pass away, but my words will never pass away.
헤번 언드 어쓰 윌 패스 어웨이, 벗 마이 워즈 윌 네버 패스 어웨이.
천지는 없어질지언정 내 말은 없어지지 아니하리라
36 "But about that day or hour no one knows, not even the angels in heaven, nor the Son, but only the Father.
벗 어바우트 댓 데이 오어 아우어 노우 원 노우즈, 낫 이빈 디 에인절즈 인 헤번, 노어 더 선, 벗 오운리 더 파더.
그러나 그 날과 그 때는 아무도 모르나니 하늘의 천사들도, 아들도 모르고 오직 아버지만 아시느니라

John 14 : 6

6 Jesus answered, "I am the way and the truth and the life. No one comes to the Father except through me.
지저스 앤서드, 아이 앰 더 웨이 언드 더 트루쓰 언드 더 라이프. 노우 원 컴즈 투 더 파더 익셉트 쓰루 미.
예수께서 이르시되 내가 곧 길이요 진리요 생명이니 나로 말미암지 않고는 아버지께로 올 자가 없느니라

Romans 1 : 2~4

2 the gospel he promised beforehand through his prophets in the Holy Scriptures
더 가스펄 히 프라머스트 비포어핸드 쓰루 히즈 프라펏스 인 더 호울리 스크립처즈
이 복음은 하나님이 선지자들을 통하여 그의 아들에 관하여 성경에 미리 약속하신 것이라

3 regarding his Son, who as to his earthly life was a descendant of David,
러가아딩 히즈 선, 후 애즈 투 히즈 어쓸리 라이프 와즈 어 디센던트 어브 데이비드,
그의 아들에 관하여 말하면 육신으로는 다윗의 혈통에서 나셨고

4 and who through the Spirit of holiness was appointed the Son of God in power by his resurrection from the dead: Jesus Christ our Lord.
언드 후 쓰루 더 스피럿 어브 호울리너스 와즈 어포인터드 더 선 어브 가드 인 파워 바이 히즈 레저렉션 프럼 더 데드 지저스 크라이스트 아우어 로어드.
성결의 영으로는 죽은 자들 가운데서 부활하사 능력으로 하나님의 아들로 선포되셨으니 곧 우리 주 예수 그리스도시니라

1 Corinthians 15 : 3~8

3 For what I received I passed on to you as of first importance: that Christ died for our sins according to the Scriptures,
포어 웟 아이 러시브드 아이 패스트 안 투 유 애즈 어브 퍼스트 임포어턴스 댓 크라이스트 다이드 포어 아우어 신즈 어코어딩 투 더 스크립처즈,
내가 받은 것을 먼저 너희에게 전하였노니 이는 성경대로 그리스도께서 우리 죄를 위하여 죽으시고

4 that he was buried, that he was raised on the third day according to the Scriptures,
댓 히 와즈 베어리드, 댓 히 와즈 레이즈드 안 더 써드 데이 어코어딩 투 더 스크립처즈,
장사 지낸 바 되셨다가 성경대로 사흘 만에 다시 살아나사

5 and that he appeared to Cephas, and then to the Twelve.
언드 댓 히 어피어드 투 세퍼즈, 언드 덴 투 더 트웰브.
게바에게 보이시고 후에 열두 제자에게와

6 After that, he appeared to more than five hundred of the brothers and sisters at the same time, most of whom are still living, though some have fallen asleep.
애프터 댓, 히 어피어드 투 모어 던 파이브 헌드러드 어브 더 브러더즈 언드 시스터즈 앳 더 세임 타임, 모우스트 어브 훔 아아 스틸 리빙, 도우 섬 해브 팔런 어슬립.
그 후에 오백여 형제에게 일시에 보이셨나니 그 중에 지금까지 대다수는 살아 있고 어떤 사람은 잠들었으며

7 Then he appeared to James, then to all the apostles,
덴 히 어피어드 투 제임즈, 덴 투 올 디 어포설즈,
그 후에 야고보에게 보이셨으며 그 후에 모든 사도에게와

8 and last of all he appeared to me also, as to one abnormally born.
언드 래스트 어브 올 히 어피어드 투 미 올소우, 애즈 투 원 애브노어멀리 본.
맨 나중에 만삭되지 못하여 난 자 같은 내게도 보이셨느니라

1 Corinthians 15 : 14~19

14 And if Christ has not been raised, our preaching is useless and so is your faith.
언드 이프 크라이스트 해즈 낫 빈 레이즈드, 아우어 프리칭 이즈 유슬러스 언드 소우 이즈 요어 페이쓰.
그리스도께서 만일 다시 살아나지 못하셨으면 우리가 전파하는 것도 헛것이요 또 너희 믿음도 헛것이며

15 More than that, we are then found to be false witnesses about God, for we have testified about God that he raised Christ from the dead. But he did not raise him if in fact the dead are not raised.
모어 던 댓, 위 아아 덴 파운드 투 비 폴스 윗너서즈 어바우트 가드, 포어 위 해브 테스티파이드 어바우트 가드 댓 히 레이즈드 크라이스트 프럼 더 데드. 벗 히 디드 낫 레이즈 힘 이프 인 팩트 더 데드 아아 낫 레이즈드.
또 우리가 하나님의 거짓 증인으로 발견되리니 우리가 하나님이 그리스도를 다시 살리셨다고 증언하였음이라 만일 죽은 자가 다시 살아나는 일이 없으면 하나님이 그리스도를 다시 살리지 아니하셨으리라

16 For if the dead are not raised, then Christ has not been raised either.
포어 이프 더 데드 아아 낫 레이즈드, 덴 크라이스트 해즈 낫 빈 레이즈드 아이더.
만일 죽은 자가 다시 살아나는 일이 없으면 그리스도도 다시 살아나신 일이 없었을 터이요
17 And if Christ has not been raised, your faith is futile; you are still in your sins.
언드 이프 크라이스트 해즈 낫 빈 레이즈드, 요어 페이쓰 이즈 퓨털 유 아아 스틸 인 요어 신즈.
그리스도께서 다시 살아나신 일이 없으면 너희의 믿음도 헛되고 너희가 여전히 죄 가운데 있을 것이요
18 Then those also who have fallen asleep in Christ are lost.
덴 도우즈 올소우 후 해브 팔런 어슬립 인 크라이스트 아아 로스트.
또한 그리스도 안에서 잠자는 자도 망하였으리니
19 If only for this life we have hope in Christ, we are of all people most to be pitied.
이프 오운리 포어 디스 라이프 위 해브 호웁 인 크라이스트, 위 아아 어브 올 피펄 모우스트 투 비 피티드.
만일 그리스도 안에서 우리가 바라는 것이 다만 이 세상의 삶뿐이면 모든 사람 가운데 우리가 더욱 불쌍한 자이리라

2 Corinthians 7 : 1

1 Therefore, since we have these promises, dear friends, let us purify ourselves from everything that contaminates body and spirit, perfecting holiness out of reverence for God.
데어포어, 신스 위 해브 디즈 프라머서즈, 디어 프렌즈, 렛 어스 퓨러파이 아우어셀브즈 프럼 에브리씽 댓 컨태머네잇스 바디 언드 스피럿, 퍼펙팅 호울리너스 아웃 어브 레버런스 포어 가드.
그런즉 사랑하는 자들아 이 약속을 가진 우리는 하나님을 두려워하는 가운데서 거룩함을 온전히 이루어 육과 영의 온갖 더러운 것에서 자신을 깨끗하게 하자

Philippians 2 : 9~11

9 Therefore God exalted him to the highest place and gave him the name that is above every name,
데어포어 가드 이그졸티드 힘 투 더 하이어스트 플레이스 언드 게이브 힘 더 네임 댓 이즈 어버브 에브리 네임,
이러므로 하나님이 그를 지극히 높여 모든 이름 위에 뛰어난 이름을 주사
10 that at the name of Jesus every knee should bow, in heaven and on earth and under the earth,
댓 앳 더 네임 어브 지저스 에브리 니 슈드 바우, 인 헤번 언드 안 어쓰 언드 언더 디 어쓰,
하늘에 있는 자들과 땅에 있는 자들과 땅 아래에 있는 자들로 모든 무릎을 예수의 이름에 꿇게 하시고
11 and every tongue acknowledge that Jesus Christ is Lord, to the glory of God the Father.
언드 에브리 텅 액날리지 댓 지저스 크라이스트 이즈 로어드, 투 더 글로어리 어브 가드 더 파더.
모든 입으로 예수 그리스도를 주라 시인하여 하나님 아버지께 영광을 돌리게 하셨느니라

Hebrews 1 : 1~3

1 In the past God spoke to our ancestors through the prophets at many times and in various ways,
인 더 패스트 가드 스포욱 투 아우어 앤세스터즈 쓰루 더 프라펏스 앳 메니 타임즈 언드 인 베어리어스 웨이즈,
옛적에 선지자들을 통하여 여러 부분과 여러 모양으로 우리 조상들에게 말씀하신 하나님이
2 but in these last days he has spoken to us by his Son, whom he appointed heir of all things, and through whom also he made the universe.
벗 인 디즈 래스트 데이즈 히 해즈 스포우컨 투 어스 바이 히즈 선, 훔 히 어포인터드 에어 어브 올 씽즈, 언드 쓰루 훔 올소우 히 메이드 더 유너버스.
이 모든 날 마지막에는 아들을 통하여 우리에게 말씀하셨으니 이 아들을 만유의 상속자로 세우시고 또 그로 말미암아 모든 세계를 지으셨느니라
3 The Son is the radiance of God's glory and the exact representation of his being, sustaining all things by his powerful word. After he had provided purification for sins, he sat down at the right hand of the Majesty in heaven.
더 선 이즈 더 레이디언스 어브 가즈 글로어리 언드 디 이그잭트 렙러젠테이션 어브 히즈 비잉, 서스테이닝 올 씽즈 바이 히즈 파워펄 워드. 애프터 히 해드 프러바이더드 퓨러퍼케이션 포어 신즈, 히 샛 다운 앳 더 라이트 핸드 어브 더 매저스티 인 헤번.
이는 하나님의 영광의 광채시요 그 본체의 형상이시라 그의 능력의 말씀으로 만물을 붙드시며 죄를 정결하게 하는 일을

하시고 높은 곳에 계신 지극히 크신 이의 우편에 앉으셨느니라

2 Peter 1 : 3~4

3 His divine power has given us everything we need for a godly life through our knowledge of him who called us by his own glory and goodness.
히즈 디바인 파워 해즈 기번 어스 에브리씽 위 니드 포어 어 가들리 라이프 쓰루 아우어 날러지 어브 힘 후 콜드 어스 바이 히즈 오운 글로어리 언드 구드너스.
그의 신기한 능력으로 생명과 경건에 속한 모든 것을 우리에게 주셨으니 이는 자기의 영광과 덕으로써 우리를 부르신 이를 앎으로 말미암음이라

4 Through these he has given us his very great and precious promises, so that through them you may participate in the divine nature, having escaped the corruption in the world caused by evil desires.
쓰루 디즈 히 해즈 기번 어스 히즈 베어리 그레이트 언드 프레셔스 프라머서즈, 소우 댓 쓰루 뎀 유 메이 파아티서페이트 인 더 디바인 네이처, 해빙 이스케입트 더 커럽션 인 더 월드 코즈드 바이 이벌 디자여즈.
이로써 그 보배롭고 지극히 큰 약속을 우리에게 주사 이 약속으로 말미암아 너희가 정욕 때문에 세상에서 썩어질 것을 피하여 신성한 성품에 참여하는 자가 되게 하려 하셨느니라

2 Peter 3 : 8~14

8 But do not forget this one thing, dear friends: With the Lord a day is like a thousand years, and a thousand years are like a day.
벗 두 낫 퍼겟 디스 원 씽, 디어 프렌즈: 윋 더 로어드 어 데이 이즈 라익 어 싸우전드 이어즈, 언드 어 싸우전드 이어즈 아아 라익 어 데이.
사랑하는 자들아 주께는 하루가 천 년 같고 천 년이 하루 같다는 이 한 가지를 잊지 말라

9 The Lord is not slow in keeping his promise, as some understand slowness. Instead he is patient with you, not wanting anyone to perish, but everyone to come to repentance.
더 로어드 이즈 낫 슬로우 인 키핑 히즈 프라머스, 애즈 섬 언더스탠드 슬로우너스. 인스테드 히 이즈 페이션트 윋 유, 낫 완팅 에니원 투 페어리쉬, 벗 에브리원 투 컴 투 리펜턴스.
주의 약속은 어떤 이들이 더디다고 생각하는 것 같이 더딘 것이 아니라 오직 주께서는 너희를 대하여 오래 참으사 아무도 멸망하지 아니하고 다 회개하기에 이르기를 원하시느니라

10 But the day of the Lord will come like a thief. The heavens will disappear with a roar; the elements will be destroyed by fire, and the earth and everything done in it will be laid bare.
벗 더 데이 어브 더 로어드 윌 컴 라익 어 씨프. 더 헤번즈 윌 디서피어 윋 어 로어 디 엘러먼트스 윌 비 디스트로이드 바이 파여, 언드 디 어쓰 언드 에브리씽 던 인 잇 윌 비 레이드 베어.
그러나 주의 날이 도둑 같이 오리니 그 날에는 하늘이 큰 소리로 떠나가고 물질이 뜨거운 불에 풀어지고 땅과 그 중에 있는 모든 일이 드러나리로다

11 Since everything will be destroyed in this way, what kind of people ought you to be? You ought to live holy and godly lives
신스 에브리씽 윌 비 디스트로이드 인 디스 웨이, 윗 카인드 어브 피펄 옷 유 투 비? 유 옷 투 리브 호울리 언드 가들리 라이브즈
이 모든 것이 이렇게 풀어지리니 너희가 어떠한 사람이 되어야 마땅하냐 거룩한 행실과 경건함으로

12 as you look forward to the day of God and speed its coming. That day will bring about the destruction of the heavens by fire, and the elements will melt in the heat.
애즈 유 룩 포어루어드 투 더 데이 어브 가드 언드 스피드 잇스 커밍. 댓 데이 윌 브링 어바우트 더 디스트럭션 어브 더 헤번즈 바이 파여, 언드 디 엘러먼트스 윌 멜트 인 더 힛.
하나님의 날이 임하기를 바라보고 간절히 사모하라 그 날에 하늘이 불에 타서 풀어지고 물질이 뜨거운 불에 녹아지려니와

13 But in keeping with his promise we are looking forward to a new heaven and a new earth, where righteousness dwells.
벗 인 키핑 윋 히즈 프라머스 위 아아 루킹 포어루어드 투 어 누 헤번 언드 어 누 어쓰, 웨어 라이처스너스 웰즈.
우리는 그의 약속대로 의가 있는 곳인 새 하늘과 새 땅을 바라보도다

14 So then, dear friends, since you are looking forward to this, make every effort to be found spotless, blameless and at peace with him.
소우 덴, 디어 프렌즈, 신스 유 아아 루킹 포어루어드 투 디스, 메익 에브리 에퍼트 투 비 파운드 스파틀러스, 블레임러스 언드 앳 피스 윋 힘.
그러므로 사랑하는 자들아 너희가 이것을 바라보나니 주 앞에서 점도 없고 흠도 없이 평강 가운데서 나타나기를 힘쓰라

scripture [skríptʃər] n. 성서	concern [kənsə́ːrn] vt. …에 관계하다	futile [fjúːtl] a. 쓸데없는, 무익한
thirsty [θə́ːrsti] a. 목마른, 갈망하는	sworn [swɔːrn] a. 맹세한	reverence [révərəns] n. 숭배, 존경
vinegar [vínigər] n. (식)초	withstand [wiðstǽnd] vt. 잘 견디다	universe [júːnəvə̀ːrs] n. 우주, 만유
soak [souk] vi. 젖다, 스미다	beforehand [bifɔ́ːrhænd] ad. 미리	radiance [réidiəns] n. 광휘, 빛남
stalk [stɔːk] n. 줄기, 가느다란 버팀	regard [rigɑ́ːrd] vt. 주목해서 보다	sustain [səstéin] vt. 떠받치다, 유지하다
hyssop [hísəp] n. 우슬초	holiness [hóulinis] n. 신성, 청렴결백	corruption [kərʌ́pʃən] n. 타락, 퇴폐
groan [groun] vi. 신음하다, 번민하다	testify [téstəfài] vi. 증명하다, 입증하다	roar [rɔːr] vi. 으르렁거리다, 고함치다

We will be with the Lord forever. 우리가 항상 주와 함께 있으리라

1 Thessalonians 4 : 16~17

16 For the Lord himself will come down from heaven, with a loud command, with the voice of the archangel and with the trumpet call of God, and the dead in Christ will rise first.
포어 더 로어드 힘셀프 윌 컴 다운 프럼 헤번, 윋 어 라우드 커맨드, 윋 더 보이스 어브 디 아아케인절 언드 윋 더 트럼펏 콜 어브 가드, 언드 더 데드 인 크라이스트 윌 라이즈 퍼스트.
주께서 호령과 천사장의 소리와 하나님의 나팔 소리로 친히 하늘로부터 강림하시리니 그리스도 안에서 죽은 자들이 먼저 일어나고
17 After that, we who are still alive and are left will be caught up together with them in the clouds to meet the Lord in the air. And so we will be with the Lord forever.
애프터 댓, 위 후 아아 스틸 얼라이브 언드 아아 레프트 윌 비 콧 업 터게더 윋 뎀 인 더 클라우즈 투 밋 더 로어드 인 디 에어. 언드 소우 위 윌 비 윋 더 로어드 퍼레버.
그 후에 우리 살아 남은 자들도 그들과 함께 구름 속으로 끌어 올려 공중에서 주를 영접하게 하시리니 그리하여 우리가 항상 주와 함께 있으리라

Luke 20 : 34~36

34 Jesus replied, "The people of this age marry and are given in marriage.
지저스 리플라이드, 더 피펄 어브 디스 에이지 메어리 언드 아아 기번 인 메어리지.
예수께서 이르시되 이 세상의 자녀들은 장가도 가고 시집도 가되
35 But those who are considered worthy of taking part in the age to come and in the resurrection from the dead will neither marry nor be given in marriage,
벗 도우즈 후 아아 컨시더드 워디 어브 테이킹 파아트 인 디 에이지 투 컴 언드 인 더 레저렉션 프럼 더 데드 윌 나이더 메어리 노어 비 기번 인 메어리지,
저 세상과 및 죽은 자 가운데서 부활함을 얻기에 합당히 여김을 받은 자들은 장가 가고 시집 가는 일이 없으며
36 and they can no longer die; for they are like the angels. They are God's children, since they are children of the resurrection.
언드 데이 캔 노우 롱거 다이 포어 데이 아아 라익 디 에인절즈. 데이 아아 가즈 칠드런, 신스 데이 아아 칠드런 어브 더 레저렉션.
그들은 다시 죽을 수도 없나니 이는 천사와 동등이요 부활의 자녀로서 하나님의 자녀임이라

John 5 : 26~29

26 For as the Father has life in himself, so he has granted the Son also to have life in himself.
포어 애즈 더 파더 해즈 라이프 인 힘셀프, 소우 히 해즈 그랜터드 더 선 올소우 투 해브 라이프 인 힘셀프.

아버지께서 자기 속에 생명이 있음 같이 아들에게도 생명을 주어 그 속에 있게 하셨고

27 And he has given him authority to judge because he is the Son of Man.
언드 히 해즈 기번 힘 어쏘러티 투 저지 비카즈 히 이즈 더 선 어브 맨.
또 인자됨으로 말미암아 심판하는 권한을 주셨느니라

28 "Do not be amazed at this, for a time is coming when all who are in their graves will hear his voice
두 낫 비 어메이즈드 앳 디스, 포어 어 타임 이즈 커밍 웬 올 후 아아 인 데어 그레이브즈 윌 히어 히즈 보이스
이를 놀랍게 여기지 말라 무덤 속에 있는 자가 다 그의 음성을 들을 때가 오나니

29 and come out—those who have done what is good will rise to live, and those who have done what is evil
will rise to be condemned.
언드 컴 아웃 도우즈 후 해브 던 웟 이즈 구드 윌 라이즈 투 리브, 언드 도우즈 후 해브 던 웟 이즈 이벌 윌 라이즈 투 비 컨뎀드.
선한 일을 행한 자는 생명의 부활로, 악한 일을 행한 자는 심판의 부활로 나오리라

John 14 : 1~3

1 "Do not let your hearts be troubled. You believe in God; believe also in me.
두 낫 렛 요어 하아트스 비 트러벌드. 유 빌리브 인 가드 빌리브 올소우 인 미.
너희는 마음에 근심하지 말라 하나님을 믿으니 또 나를 믿으라

2 My Father's house has many rooms; if that were not so, would I have told you that I am going there to
prepare a place for you ?
마이 파더즈 하우스 해즈 메니 룸즈 이프 댓 워 낫 소우, 워드 아이 해브 토울드 유 댓 아이 앰 고우잉 데어 투 프리페어 어 플레이스 포어 유?
내 아버지 집에 거할 곳이 많도다 그렇지 않으면 너희에게 일렀으리라 내가 너희를 위하여 거처를 예비하러 가노니

3 And if I go and prepare a place for you, I will come back and take you to be with me that you also may be
where I am.
언드 이프 아이 고우 언드 프리페어 어 플레이스 포어 유, 아이 윌 컴 백 언드 테익 유 투 비 윋 미 댓 유 올소우 메이비 웨어 아이 앰.
가서 너희를 위하여 거처를 예비하면 내가 다시 와서 너희를 내게로 영접하여 나 있는 곳에 너희도 있게 하리라

Romans 6 : 10~11

10 The death he died, he died to sin once for all; but the life he lives, he lives to God.
더 데쓰 히 다이드, 히 다이드 투 신 원스 포어 올 벗 더 라이프 히 리브즈, 히 리브즈 투 가드.
그가 죽으심은 죄에 대하여 단번에 죽으심이요 그가 살아 계심은 하나님께 대하여 살아 계심이니

11 In the same way, count yourselves dead to sin but alive to God in Christ Jesus.
인 더 세임 웨이, 카운트 유어셀브즈 데드 투 신 벗 얼라이브 투 가드 인 크라이스트 지저스.
이와 같이 너희도 너희 자신을 죄에 대하여는 죽은 자요 그리스도 예수 안에서 하나님께 대하여는 살아 있는 자로 여길지어다

1 Corinthians 9 : 25~27

25 Everyone who competes in the games goes into strict training. They do it to get a crown that will not
last, but we do it to get a crown that will last forever.
에브리원 후 컴핏스 인 더 게임즈 고우즈 인투 스트릭트 트레이닝. 데이 두 잇 투 겟 어 크라운 댓 윌 낫 래스트, 벗 위 두 잇 투 겟 어 크라운 댓 윌 래스트 퍼레버.
이기기를 다투는 자마다 모든 일에 절제하나니 그들은 썩을 승리자의 관을 얻고자 하되 우리는 썩지 아니할 것을 얻고자 하노라

26 Therefore I do not run like someone running aimlessly; I do not fight like a boxer beating the air.
데어포어 아이 두 낫 런 라익 서뭔 러닝 에임러슬리 아이 두 낫 파이트 라익 어 박서 비팅 디 에어.
그러므로 나는 달음질하기를 향방 없는 것 같이 아니하고 싸우기를 허공을 치는 것 같이 아니하며

27 No, I strike a blow to my body and make it my slave so that after I have preached to others, I myself will

not be disqualified for the prize.
노우, 아이 스트라익 어 블로우 투 마이 바디 언드 메익 잇 마이 슬레이브 소우 댓 애프터 아이 해브 프리치트 투 어더즈, 아이 마이셀프 윌 낫 비 디스콸러파이드 포어 더 프라이즈.
내가 내 몸을 쳐 복종하게 함은 내가 남에게 전파한 후에 자신이 도리어 버림을 당할까 두려워함이로다

1 Corinthians 15 : 20~22

20 But Christ has indeed been raised from the dead, the firstfruits of those who have fallen asleep.
벗 크라이스트 해즈 인디드 빈 레이즈드 프럼 더 데드, 더 퍼스트프룻스 어브 도우즈 후 해브 팔런 어슬립.
그러나 이제 그리스도께서 죽은 자 가운데서 다시 살아나사 잠자는 자들의 첫 열매가 되셨도다
21 For since death came through a man, the resurrection of the dead comes also through a man.
포어 신스 데쓰 케임 쓰루 어 맨, 더 레저렉션 어브 더 데드 컴즈 올소우 쓰루 어 맨.
사망이 한 사람으로 말미암았으니 죽은 자의 부활도 한 사람으로 말미암는도다
22 For as in Adam all die, so in Christ all will be made alive.
포어 애즈 인 애덤 올 다이, 소우 인 크라이스트 올 윌 비 메이드 얼라이브.
아담 안에서 모든 사람이 죽은 것 같이 그리스도 안에서 모든 사람이 삶을 얻으리라

Philippians 3 : 13~14

13 Brothers and sisters, I do not consider myself yet to have taken hold of it. But one thing I do: Forgetting what is behind and straining toward what is ahead,
브러더즈 언드 시스터즈, 아이 두 낫 컨시더 마이셀프 옛 투 해브 테이컨 호울드 어브 잇. 벗 원 씽 아이 두 퍼게팅 웟 이즈 비하인드 언드 스트레이닝 터워어드 웟 이즈 어헤드,
형제들아 나는 아직 내가 잡은 줄로 여기지 아니하고 오직 한 일 즉 뒤에 있는 것은 잊어버리고 앞에 있는 것을 잡으려고
14 I press on toward the goal to win the prize for which God has called me heavenward in Christ Jesus.
아이 프레스 안 터워어드 더 고울 투 윈 더 프라이즈 포어 위치 가드 해즈 콜드 미 헤버느워드 인 크라이스트 지저스.
푯대를 향하여 그리스도 예수 안에서 하나님이 위에서 부르신 부름의 상을 위하여 달려가노라

Titus 2 : 12~14

12 It teaches us to say "No" to ungodliness and worldly passions, and to live self-controlled, upright and godly lives in this present age,
잇 티처즈 어스 투 세이 노우 투 언고들리너스 언드 월들리 패션즈, 언드 투 리브 셀프컨트로울드, 업라이트 언드 가들리 라이브즈 인 디스 프레전트 에이지,
우리를 양육하시되 경건하지 않은 것과 이 세상 정욕을 다 버리고 신중함과 의로움과 경건함으로 이 세상에 살고
13 while we wait for the blessed hope—the appearing of the glory our great God and Savior, Jesus Christ,
와일 위 웨잇 포어 더 블레스트 호웁 디 어피링 어브 더 글로어리 아우어 그레이트 가드 언드 세이브여, 지저스 크라이스트,
복스러운 소망과 우리의 크신 하나님 구주 예수 그리스도의 영광이 나타나심을 기다리게 하셨으니
14 who gave himself for us to redeem us from all wickedness and to purify for himself a people that are his very own, eager to do what is good.
후 게이브 힘셀프 포어 어스 투 리딤 어스 프럼 올 위커드너스 언드 투 퓨러파이 포어 힘셀프 어 피펄 댓 아아 히즈 베어리 오운, 이거 투 두 웟 이즈 구드.
그가 우리를 대신하여 자신을 주심은 모든 불법에서 우리를 속량하시고 우리를 깨끗하게 하사 선한 일을 열심히 하는 자기 백성이 되게 하려 하심이라

Titus 3 : 4~7

4 But when the kindness and love of God our Savior appeared,
벗 웬 더 카인드너스 언드 러브 어브 가드 아우어 세이브여 어피어드,
우리 구주 하나님의 자비와 사람 사랑하심이 나타날 때에
5 he saved us, not because of righteous things we had done, but because of his mercy. He saved us through the washing of rebirth and renewal by the Holy Spirit,
히 세이브드 어스, 낫 비카즈 어브 라이처스 씽즈 위 해드 던, 벗 비카즈 어브 히즈 머시. 히 세이브드 어스 쓰루 더 와싱 어

브 리버쓰 언드 리누얼 바이 더 호울리 스피릿,
우리를 구원하시되 우리가 행한 바 의로운 행위로 말미암지 아니하고 오직 그의 긍휼하심을 따라 중생의 씻음과 성령의 새롭게 하심으로 하셨나니

6 whom he poured out on us generously through Jesus Christ our Savior,
훔 히 포어드 아웃 안 어스 제너러슬리 쓰루 지저스 크라이스트 아우어 세이브여,
우리 구주 예수 그리스도로 말미암아 우리에게 그 성령을 풍성히 부어 주사

7 so that, having been justified by his grace, we might become heirs having the hope of eternal life.
소우 댓, 해빙 빈 저스터파이드 바이 히즈 그레이스, 위 마이트 비컴 에어즈 해빙 더 호웁 어브 이터널 라이프.
우리로 그의 은혜를 힘입어 의롭다 하심을 얻어 영생의 소망을 따라 상속자가 되게 하려 하심이라

Hebrews 4 : 10~14

10 for anyone who enters God's rest also rests from their works, just as God did from his.
포어 에니원 후 엔터즈 가즈 레스트 올소우 레스트스 프럼 데어 웍스, 저스트 애즈 가드 디드 프럼 히즈.
이미 그의 안식에 들어간 자는 하나님이 자기의 일을 쉬심과 같이 그도 자기의 일을 쉬느니라

11 Let us, therefore, make every effort to enter that rest, so that no one will perish by following their example of disobedience.
렛 어스, 데어포어, 메익 에브리 에퍼트 투 엔터 댓 레스트, 소우 댓 노우 원 윌 페어리쉬 바이 팔로우잉 데어 이그잼펄 어브 디서비디언스.
그러므로 우리가 저 안식에 들어가기를 힘쓸지니 이는 누구든지 저 순종하지 아니하는 본에 빠지지 않게 하려 함이라

12 For the word of God is alive and active. Sharper than any double-edged sword, it penetrates even to dividing soul and spirit, joints and marrow; it judges the thoughts and attitudes of the heart.
포어 더 워드 어브 가드 이즈 얼라이브 언드 액티브. 샤아퍼 던 에니 더벌에지드 소어드, 잇 페넛레잇스 이빈 투 디바이딩 소울 언드 스피릿, 조인트스 언드 메어로우 잇 저지즈 더 쏫스 언드 애터투즈 어브 더 하아트.
하나님의 말씀은 살아 있고 활력이 있어 좌우에 날선 어떤 검보다도 예리하여 혼과 영과 및 관절과 골수를 찔러 쪼개기까지 하며 또 마음의 생각과 뜻을 판단하나니

13 Nothing in all creation is hidden from God's sight. Everything is uncovered and laid bare before the eyes of him to whom we must give account.
너씽 인 올 크리에이션 이즈 히던 프럼 가즈 사이트. 에브리씽 이즈 언커버드 언드 레이드 베어 비포어 디 아이즈 어브 힘 투 훔 위 머스트 기브 어카운트.
지으신 것이 하나도 그 앞에 나타나지 않음이 없고 우리의 결산을 받으실 이의 눈 앞에 만물이 벌거벗은 것 같이 드러나느니라

14 Therefore, since we have a great high priest who has ascended into heaven, Jesus the Son of God, let us hold firmly to the faith we profess.
데어포어, 신스 위 해브 어 그레이트 하이 프리스트 후 해즈 어센더드 인투 헤번, 지저스 더 선 어브 가드, 렛 어스 호울드 펌리 투 더 페이쓰 위 프러페스.
그러므로 우리에게 큰 대제사장이 계시니 승천하신 이 곧 하나님의 아들 예수시라 우리가 믿는 도리를 굳게 잡을지어다

Hebrews 6 : 17~20

17 Because God wanted to make the unchanging nature of his purpose very clear to the heirs of what was promised, he confirmed it with an oath.
비카즈 가드 원티드 투 메익 디 언체인징 네이처 어브 히즈 퍼퍼스 베어리 클리어 투 디 에어즈 어브 윗 와즈 프라머스트, 히 컨펌드 잇 윋 앤 오우쓰.
하나님은 약속을 기업으로 받는 자들에게 그 뜻이 변하지 아니함을 충분히 나타내시려고 그 일을 맹세로 보증하셨나니

18 God did this so that, by two unchangeable things in which it is impossible for God to lie, we who have fled to take hold of the hope set before us may be greatly encouraged.
가드 디드 디스 소우 댓, 바이 투 언체인저벌 씽즈 인 위치 잇 이즈 임파서벌 포어 가드 투 라이, 위 후 해브 플레드 투 테익 호울드 어브 더 호웁 셋 비포어 어스 메이 비 그레잇리 인커러지드.
이는 하나님이 거짓말을 하실 수 없는 이 두 가지 변하지 못할 사실로 말미암아 앞에 있는 소망을 얻으려고 피난처를 찾

은 우리에게 큰 안위를 받게 하려 하심이라

19 We have this hope as an anchor for the soul, firm and secure. It enters the inner sanctuary behind the curtain,
위 해브 디스 호웁 애즈 앤 앵커 포어 더 소울, 펌 언드 시큐. 잇 엔터즈 디 이너 생크추에어리 비하인드 더 커턴,
우리가 이 소망을 가지고 있는 것은 영혼의 닻 같아서 튼튼하고 견고하여 휘장 안에 들어 가나니

20 where our forerunner, Jesus, has entered on our behalf. He has become a high priest forever, in the order of Melchizedek.
웨어 아우어 포러너, 지저스, 해즈 엔터드 안 아우어 비해프. 히 해즈 비컴 어 하이 프리스트 퍼레버, 인 디 오어더 어브 메일치즈딕.
그리로 앞서 가신 예수께서 멜기세덱의 반차를 따라 영원히 대제사장이 되어 우리를 위하여 들어 가셨느니라

Hebrews 9 : 27~28

27 Just as people are destined to die once, and after that to face judgment,
저스트 애즈 피펄 아아 데스틴드 투 다이 원스, 언드 애프터 댓 투 페이스 저지먼트,
한번 죽는 것은 사람에게 정해진 것이요 그 후에는 심판이 있으리니

28 so Christ was sacrificed once to take away the sins of many; and he will appear a second time, not to bear sin, but to bring salvation to those who are waiting for him.
소우 크라이스트 와즈 새크러파이스트 원스 투 테익 어웨이 더 신즈 어브 메니 언드 히 윌 어피어 어 세컨드 타임, 낫 투 베어 신, 벗 투 브링 샐베이션 투 도우즈 후 아아 웨이팅 포어 힘.
이와 같이 그리스도도 많은 사람의 죄를 담당하시려고 단번에 드리신 바 되셨고 구원에 이르게 하기 위하여 죄와 상관 없이 자기를 바라는 자들에게 두 번째 나타나시리라

1 Peter 1 : 2~4

2 who have been chosen according to the foreknowledge of God the Father, through the sanctifying work of the Spirit, to be obedient to Jesus Christ and sprinkled with his blood: Grace and peace be yours in abundance.
후 해브 빈 초우전 어코어딩 투 더 포어크날리지 어브 가드 더 파더, 쓰루 더 생크터파이잉 웍 어브 더 스피릿, 투 비 오우비디언트 투 지저스 크라이스트 언드 스프링컬드 윋 히즈 블러드 그레이스 언드 피스 비 유어즈 인 어번던스.
곧 하나님 아버지의 미리 아심을 따라 성령이 거룩하게 하심으로 순종함과 예수 그리스도의 피 뿌림을 얻기 위하여 택하심을 받은 자들에게 편지하노니 은혜와 평강이 너희에게 더욱 많을지어다

3 Praise be to the God and Father of our Lord Jesus Christ! In his great mercy he has given us new birth into a living hope through the resurrection of Jesus Christ from the dead,
프레이즈 비 투 더 가드 언드 파더 어브 아우어 로어드 지저스 크라이스트! 인 히즈 그레이트 머시 히 해즈 기번 어스 누 버쓰 인투 어 리빙 호웁 쓰루 더 레저렉션 어브 지저스 크라이스트 프럼 더 데드,
우리 주 예수 그리스도의 아버지 하나님을 찬송하리로다 그의 많으신 긍휼대로 예수 그리스도를 죽은 자 가운데서 부활하게 하심으로 말미암아 우리를 거듭나게 하사 산 소망이 있게 하시며

4 and into an inheritance that can never perish, spoil or fade. This inheritance is kept in heaven for you,
언드 인투 앤 인헤러턴스 댓 캔 네버 페어리쉬, 스포일 오어 페이드. 디스 인헤러턴스 이즈 켑트 인 헤번 포어 유,
썩지 않고 더럽지 않고 쇠하지 아니하는 유업을 잇게 하시나니 곧 너희를 위하여 하늘에 간직하신 것이라

1 Peter 1 : 18~21

18 For you know that it was not with perishable things such as silver or gold that you were redeemed from the empty way of life handed down to you from your ancestors,
포어 유 노우 댓 잇 와즈 낫 윋 페어리셔벌 씽즈 서치 애즈 실버 오어 고울드 댓 유 워 리딤드 프럼 디 엠프티 웨이 어브 라이프 핸더드 다운 투 유 프럼 요어 앤세스터즈,
너희가 알거니와 너희 조상이 물려 준 헛된 행실에서 대속함을 받은 것은 은이나 금 같이 없어질 것으로 된 것이 아니요

19 but with the precious blood of Christ, a lamb without blemish or defect.
벗 윋 더 프레셔스 블러드 어브 크라이스트, 어 램 위다우트 블레미쉬 오어 디펙트.
오직 흠 없고 점 없는 어린 양 같은 그리스도의 보배로운 피로 된 것이니라

20 He was chosen before the creation of the world, but was revealed in these last times for your sake.

히 와즈 초우전 비포어 더 크리에이션 어브 더 월드, 벗 와즈 리빌드 인 디즈 래스트 타임즈 포어 요어 세익.
그는 창세 전부터 미리 알린 바 되신 이나 이 말세에 너희를 위하여 나타내신 바 되었으니

21 Through him you believe in God, who raised him from the dead and glorified him, and so your faith
and hope are in God.
쓰루 힘 유 빌리브 인 가드, 후 레이즈드 힘 프럼 더 데드 언드 글로어러파이드 힘, 언드 소우 요어 페이쓰 언드 호웁 아아
인 가드.
너희는 그를 죽은 자 가운데서 살리시고 영광을 주신 하나님을 그리스도로 말미암아 믿는 자니 너희 믿음과 소망이 하나
님께 있게 하셨느니라

1 John 3 : 2~3

2 Dear friends, now we are children of God, and what we will be has not yet been made known. But we
know that when Christ appears, we shall be like him, for we shall see him as he is.
디어 프렌즈, 나우 위 아아 칠드런 어브 가드, 언드 윗 위 윌 비 해즈 낫 옛 빈 메이드 노운. 벗 위 노우 댓 웬 크라이스트 어
피어즈, 위 섈 비 라익 힘, 포어 위 섈 시 힘 애즈 히 이즈.
사랑하는 자들아 우리가 지금은 하나님의 자녀라 장래에 어떻게 될지는 아직 나타나지 아니하였으나 그가 나타나시면 우
리가 그와 같을 줄을 아는 것은 그의 참모습 그대로 볼 것이기 때문이니

3 All who have this hope in him purify themselves, just as he is pure.
올 후 해브 디스 호웁 인 힘 퓨러파이 뎀셀브즈, 저스트 애즈 히 이즈 퓨.
주를 향하여 이 소망을 가진 자마다 그의 깨끗하심과 같이 자기를 깨끗하게 하느니라

Revelation 10 : 5~7

5 Then the angel I had seen standing on the sea and on the land raised his right hand to heaven.
덴 디 에인절 아이 해드 신 스탠딩 안 더 시 언드 안 더 랜드 레이즈드 히즈 라이트 핸드 투 헤번.
내가 본 바 바다와 땅을 밟고 서 있는 천사가 하늘을 향하여 오른손을 들고

6 And he swore by him who lives for ever and ever, who created the heavens and all that is in them, the
earth and all that is in it, and the sea and all that is in it, and said, "There will be no more delay!
언드 히 스워어 바이 힘 후 리브즈 포어 에버 언드 에버, 후 크리에이터드 더 헤번즈 언드 올 댓 이즈 인 뎀, 디 어쓰 언드 올
댓 이즈 인 잇, 언드 더 시 언드 올 댓 이즈 인 잇, 언드 세드, 데어 윌 비 노우 모어 딜레이!
세세토록 살아 계신 이 곧 하늘과 그 가운데에 있는 물건이며 땅과 그 가운데에 있는 물건이며 바다와 그 가운데에 있는
물건을 창조하신 이를 가리켜 맹세하여 이르되 지체하지 아니하리니

7 But in the days when the seventh angel is about to sound his trumpet, the mystery of God will be accom-
plished, just as he announced to his servants the prophets."
벗 인 더 데이즈 웬 더 세 번쓰 에인절 이즈 어바우트 투 사운드 히즈 트럼펏, 더 미스터리 어브 가드 윌 비 어캄플리쉬트,
저스트 애즈 히 어나운스트 투 히즈 서번트스 더 프라펏스.
일곱째 천사가 소리 내는 날 그의 나팔을 불려고 할 때에 하나님이 그의 종 선지자들에게 전하신 복음과 같이 하나님의 그
비밀이 이루어지리라 하더라

archangel [ɑ́ːrkèindʒəl] n. 대천사
consider [kənsídər] vt. 숙고하다
compete [kəmpíːt] vi. 겨루다, 경쟁하다
aimless [éimlis] a. 목적없는, 정처 없는
disqualify [diskwɑ́ləfài] vt. 실격시키다
prize [praiz] n. 상품, 상
indeed [indíːd] ad. 실로, 참으로
strain [strein] vt. 잡아당기다, 꽉 죄다
passion [pǽʃən] n. 열정, 격노
redeem [ridíːm] vt. 사다, 상환하다
rebirth [riːbɜːrθ] n. 재생, 갱생
generous [dʒénərəs] a. 후한, 푸짐한
disobedience [dìsəbíːdiəns] n. 불순종
penetrate [pénətrèit] vt. 꿰뚫다
anchor [ǽŋkər] n. 닻
sanctuary [sǽŋktʃuèri] n. 거룩한 장소
forerunner [fɔ́ːrrʌ̀nər] n. 선구자
foreknowledge [fɔːrnɑ́lidʒ] n. 예지, 통찰
sprinkle [spríŋkəl] vt. 뿌리다, 끼얹다
blemish [blémiʃ] n. 흠, 오점, 결점
announce [ənáuns] vt. 알리다

도서출판 사랑의장막 저서들

분별과 투시로 열리는 영적세계

저자 김다윗

우상 숭배와 음란으로 실패하는 삶의 원인을
규명해 주고 승리의 삶으로 이끌어주는 안내서이다.

14차원으로 열리는 성령의 세계 – 제1권 불의 4차원

저자 김다윗

하나님의 자녀로서 권세 있는 삶을 살아가는 비결은 오직 성령의
충만함에 있다. 이 책은 깊은 기도의 영성으로 열리는 성령의
3속성을 14단계로 풀어 쉽게 이해할 수 있도록 설명하고 있다.

사랑하는 사람들을 향한 사랑의 노래

저자 이해경

시집으로 자녀를 향한 사랑의 노래, 남편과 아내를 향한
사랑의 노래, 하나님을 향한 사랑의 노래, 비전을 향한
사랑의 노래가 수록되어 있다.

개역개정 지혜의 성경 잠언 따라쓰기

사랑의장막 편집부

잠언은 우리 자녀들을 명철하며, 지혜롭게,
공의롭게, 정의롭게, 정직하게 자라나게 합니다.

개역개정 약속의 성경 요절 따라쓰기

사랑의장막 편집부

성경은 하나님의 약속으로 가득합니다. 약속의 성경 요절따라쓰기는
우리 자녀들이 예수님을 믿는 믿음 안에서 천국에 대한 확실한 소망을
가지고 살아가기를 바라는 마음으로 만든 책입니다.

NIV개정 지혜의 성경 영어잠언 따라쓰기 1, 2 (전 2권)

사랑의장막 편집부

영어잠언 따라쓰기를 쓰면서 좋은 영어 글씨체를 갖게 되고,
원어민 발음과 한국어 성경(개역개정)을 수록하여 영어 잠언이 쉽게
읽어집니다. 또한 각 페이지마다 숙어와 예문, 각 장마다 단어를 정리하여
영어 해석에 도움이 됩니다.

NIV개정 약속의 성경 영어 요절 따라쓰기

사랑의장막 편집부

성경은 하나님의 약속으로 가득합니다. 약속의 성경 영어요절 따라쓰기는
약속의 성경 요절 따라쓰기를 영어판(NIV개정)으로 만든 것입니다. 하나님
의 약속들을 마음판에 새기며, 천국에 대한 확실한 소망을 가지고 세상에
서 성령의 능력으로 빛과 소금이 되기를 원합니다.